FLOWER & HAND

OTHER BOOKS OF POETRY BY W. S. MERWIN

A Mask for Janus (1952)
The Dancing Bears (1954)
Green With Beasts (1956)
The Drunk in the Furnace (1960)
The Moving Target (1963)
The Lice (1967)
The Carrier of Ladders (1970)
Writings to an Unfinished Accompaniment (1973)
The First Four Books of Poems (1975)
The Compass Flower (1977)
Finding the Islands (1982)
Opening the Hand (1983)
The Rain in the Trees (1988)
Selected Poems (1988)
Travels (1993)
The Second Four Books of Poems (Copper Canyon Press, 1993)
The Vixen (1996)

W.S. MERWIN

Flower & Hand

POEMS 1977–1983

The Compass Flower

Opening the Hand

Feathers from the Hill

COPPER CANYON PRESS

Publication of this book is supported by a grant from the National Endowment for the Arts and a grant from the Lannan Foundation. Additional support to Copper Canyon Press has been provided by the Andrew W. Mellon Foundation, the Lila Wallace–Reader's Digest Fund, and the Washington State Arts Commission. Copper Canyon Press is in residence with Centrum at Fort Worden State Park.

Library of Congress Cataloging-in-Publication Data
Merwin, W. S. (William Stanley), 1927–
Flower & hand : poems 1977–1983 / by W. S. Merwin.
p. cm.
ISBN 1-55659-119-5
I. Title. II. Title: Flower and hand.
PS3563.E75F55 1997
811'.54 – dc20   96-35616

COPPER CANYON PRESS
P.O. BOX 271, PORT TOWNSEND, WASHINGTON 98368

CONTENTS

The Compass Flower (1977)

I

II

Feathers from the Hill (1978)

Opening the Hand (1983)

I

I I

III

THE COMPASS FLOWER

(1977)

I

The Heart

In the first chamber of the heart
all the gloves are hanging but two
the hands are bare as they come through the door
the bell rope is moving without them
they move forward cupped as though
holding water
there is a bird a thing in their palms
in this chamber there is no color

In the second chamber of the heart
all the blindfolds are hanging but one
the eyes are open as they come in
they see the bell rope moving
without hands
they see the bathing bird
being carried forward
through the colored chamber

In the third chamber of the heart
all the sounds are hanging but one
the ears hear nothing as they come through the door
the bell rope is moving like a breath
without hands
a bird is being carried forward
bathing
in total silence

In the last chamber of the heart
all the words are hanging
but one
the blood is naked as it steps through the door
with its eyes open
and a bathing bird in its hands
and with its bare feet on the sill

moving as though on water
to the one stroke of the bell
someone is ringing without hands

The Wine

With what joy I am carrying
a case of wine up a mountain
far behind me others
are being given their burdens
but I could not wait even for them

it is wine that I will not drink
I will not drink it not I
this wine
a signpost is swinging around
up in the woods in the fog
one way saying Almost one way Punished
in another language that I know
but no sign this way

by now all the stone railing
is fog
no longer does the dew brushed
from the pine needles onto my fingers
run down into my armpits
how cold my hands are
how awkward the wine is to carry
on my shoulder
that's part of the joy

The Drive Home

I was always afraid
of the time when I would arrive home
and be met by a special car
but this wasn't like that
they were so nice the young couple
and I was relieved not to be driving
so I could see the autumn leaves on the farms

I sat in the front to see better
they sat in the back
having a good time
and they laughed with their collars up
they said we could take turns driving
but when I looked
none of us was driving

then we all laughed
we wondered if anyone would notice
we talked of getting an inflatable
driver
to drive us for nothing through the autumn leaves

The Next Moon

A month to the hour
since the last ear on earth
heard your voice

even then on the phone

I know the words about rest
and how you would say them
as though I myself had heard them

not long ago
but for a month I have heard nothing

and in the evening after the moon of deafness
I set foot in the proud waters
of iron and misfortune
it is a month to the hour
since you died
and it was only dusk
to the east in the garden

now it is a night street with another moon
seen for the first time but no longer new
and faces from the backs of mirrors

The Snow

You with no fear of dying
how you dreaded winter
the cataract forming on the green wheated hill
ice on sundial and steps and calendar
it is snowing
after you were unborn it was my turn
to carry you in a world before me
trying to imagine you
I am your parent at the beginning of winter
you are my child
we are one body
one blood
one red line melting the snow
unbroken line in falling snow

The Arrival

From many boats
ferries and borrowed canoes
white steamers and resurrected hulls
in which we were young together
to a shore older than waiting
and our feet on the wet shadowed sand
early in the evening of every verb
both of us at the foot of the mountain laughing

now will you lead me with the smell of almonds
up over the leafless mountain
in the blood red evening
now we pull up the keel through the rushes
on the beach
my feet miss the broken bottle
half buried in the sand
you did not notice it at last

now will you lead with your small hand
your child up the leafless mountain
past the green wooden doors thrown away
and abandoned shelters
into the meadows of loose horses
that I will ride in the dark to come

Apples

Waking beside a pile of unsorted keys
in an empty room
the sun is high

what a long jagged string of broken bird song
they must have made as they gathered there

by the ears deaf with sleep
and the hands empty as waves
I remember the birds now
but where are the locks

when I touch the pile
my hand sounds like a wave on a shingle beach
I hear someone stirring
in the ruins of a glass mountain
after decades

those keys are so cold that they melt at my touch
all but the one
to the door of a cold morning
the colors of apples

An Encampment at Morning

A migrant tribe of spiders
spread tents at dusk in the rye stubble
come day I see the color
of the planet under their white-beaded tents
where the spiders are bent
by shade fires in damp September
to their live instruments
and I see the color of the planet
when their tents go from above it
as I come that way in a breath cloud
learning my steps
among the tents rising invisibly like the shapes of snowflakes
we are words on a journey
not the inscriptions of settled people

Migration

Prayers of many summers come
to roost on a moment
until it sinks under them
and they resume their journey
flying by night
with the sound
of blood rushing in an ear

November

The landscape
of a link disappearing between species
and phyla
and kingdoms
is here
after what we have said good-bye to
and before what we will not be here to see
only we know this
as we are
the earth sealed with tar
the walls climbing
the feathers warm around the heart
the memory of unmarked woods
standing facing something we cannot see
exchanging familiar speech
archaic greetings of those who reappear

The Horse

In a dead tree
there is the ghost of a horse
no horse

was ever seen near the tree
but the tree was born
of a mare
it rolled with long legs
in rustling meadows
it pricked its ears
it reared and tossed its head
and suddenly stood still
beginning to remember
as its leaves fell

A Contemporary

What if I came down now out of these
solid dark clouds that build up against the mountain
day after day with no rain in them
and lived as one blade of grass
in a garden in the south when the clouds part in winter
from the beginning I would be older than all the animals
and to the last I would be simpler
frost would design me and dew would disappear on me
sun would shine through me
I would be green with white roots
feel worms touch my feet as a bounty
have no name and no fear
turn naturally to the light
know how to spend the day and night
climbing out of myself
all my life

Fishing

Day and night as a child
I could imagine feeling the bite on the line
moment of fire
above a drum of white
stone water
with the line vibrating through it
one-string harp
never to be out of the feeling in my fingers
name from before anyone was born
bright color in darkness through half a life
beating suddenly toward me

Guardians

Fine rain drifts along mountains to the south of me
graying the first month
one migrant bird scolding in misted noon
in the pear tree
dogs yapping beyond mud walls
echoing back and forth wooden bells
who is listening
eight sacred fears keep watch over me
behind each of them one of the porches of dissolution
in the place of the ninth an open gate
each of them holds the end of one strand
of a rope made of the eight ribs of the world
which leads through the fearless gate

the swan drifts over mountains to the south of me
in the first month
and in the white cloud small birds begin to sing
hair-roots of trees stir

fear is one aspect of joyful guardians
because of the way I came
and clearly I have been in love with some of them
with her who is Fear of the Journey
who has repeatedly and faithfully led me
most of them I cannot even see
in the white sky over my travelling cradle
watching me
ready to bear me up in ageless hands
of cloud and glass
for as long as I need them

Fate

Cloud in the morning
evening a white opal
after a white sun
the lighted opal sits on the rim
of dark mountains
some are born hearing dogs bark in the mountains
among high walls just after sunset
and all their lives things are known to them
that are not known even to those born hearing water
or trees or sobbing or flutes or laughing

On the Mountain

A wind at first light
comes out of one
waving pine tree
air river too deep to be seen
current with no surface
then can be heard and felt

it carries deep reflections of birds
and of sunrise clouds
thoughts into the sea of day

Vision

What is unseen
flows to what is unseen
passing in part
through what we partly see
we stood up from all fours
far back in the light
to look
as long as there is day
and part of the night

The Deluge

Before there was a body
an eye wandered in a forest
to see how it would be
only when the trees were gone
did the veins appear
newly joined and windowed
and the eye embarked in the body
one of an only pair
on the rising waters
to watch for the end of the rain
of age

Robin

In one of the creations
the robin invented
the day
in order to escape from the owl
and they
killed cock robin
and he entered the next world
when the world he knew was utterly destroyed
many worlds before ours
and he invented the day
for a new reason
and again we survived
we survivors
without knowing why

II

City

I have been here before
I have entered through a glass door
at the end of a corridor
surprised to find nothing locked
but knowing that someone was watching
I have arrived through a hospital
I have steered in through the tightening outskirts
in the morning crowd
I have undergone inspections been counted have believed
I have learned the streets like seasons
I have forgotten whole years
but never have I seen it with so few people showing
not even at this hour before daylight so little traffic
never so like held breath
all the traffic lights dark
never such temptation to drive too fast

Line

Those waiting in line
for a cash register at a supermarket
pushing wire baby carriages
full of food in packages
past signs about coupons
in the blank light
do not look at each other
frankly
pretend not to stare at each other's
soft drinks and white bread
do not think of themselves as
part of a line
ordinarily
and the clerk often does not

look at them
giving them change
and the man who puts the things
they have chosen
into bags
talks to the clerk
as he never talks to her
at any other time

The Estuary

By day we pace the many decks
of the stone boat
and at night we are turned out in its high windows
like stars of another side
taste our mouths we are the salt of the earth
salt is memory
in storm and cloud
we sleep in fine rigging like riding birds
taste our fingers
each with its own commandment
day or night it is harder to know than we know
but longer
we are asleep over charts at running windows
we are asleep with compasses in our hands
and at the bow of the stone boat
the wave from the ends of the earth keeps breaking

The Rock

Saxophone and subway
under waking and sleeping
then few hundred feet down nobody

sound of inner stone
with heart on fire

on top of it where it would dream
in the light on its head
and in its shadow
we know one another
riding deaf together
flying up in boxes
through gray gases
and here pause
to breathe

all
our walls shake if we
listen
if we stop even
to rest a hand on them

when we can love it happens here too
where we tremble
who also are running like white grass
where sirens bleed through us
wires reach to us
we are bottles smashing in paper bags
and at the same time live standing in many windows
hearing under the breath the stone
that is ours alone

The Counting Houses

Where do the hours of a city begin and end
among so many
the limits rising
and setting each time in each body

in a city how many hands of timepieces
must be counting the hours
clicking at a given moment
numbering insects into machines to be codified
calculating newsprint in the days of the living
all together they are not infinite
any more than the ignored patience
of rubber tires day and night
or the dumbness of wheels or the wires of passions

where is the horizon the avenue has not reached it
reaching and reaching lying palm upward
exposing the places where blood is given or let
at night the veins of the sleepers remember trees
countless sleepers the hours of trees
the uncounted hours the leaves in the dark
by day the light of the streets is the color of arms kept covered
and of much purpose
again at night the lights of the streets play on ceilings
they brush across walls
of room after unlit room hung with pictures
of the youth of the world

The Helmsmen

The navigator of day
plots his way by a few
daytime stars
which he never sees
except as black calculations
on white paper
worked out to the present
and even beyond
on a single plane
while on the same breathing voyage

the other navigator steers only
by what he sees
and he names for the visions of day
what he makes out in the dark void
over his head
he names for what he has never seen
what he will never see
and he never sees
the other
the earth itself is always between them
yet he leaves messages
concerning celestial bodies
as though he were telling of his own life
and in turn he finds
messages concerning
unseen motions of celestial bodies
movements of days of a life
and both navigators call out
passing the same places as the sunrise
and the sunset
waking and sleeping they call
but can't be sure whether they hear
increasingly they imagine echoes
year after year they
try to meet
thinking of each other constantly
and of the rumors of resemblances between them

Numbered Apartment

In every room rubber bands turn up loose
on dusty surfaces
witnesses

travellers in stop-over countries
not knowing a word of the language
each of them
something in particular to do with me
who say laughing that I
was born here one William
on the last day of one September

to whom now it is again a January a Thursday
of an eleven year and
who has forgotten that
day and to whom that week is inaccessible
and this one is plain this
one

and though I say
here
I know it was not
for even at that time it was
ninety-nine streets to the north by the river
and now it is three wars back
and parents gone as though at once

the edifice in the antique
mode of kings of France
to which they took her to give birth
torn down as I
in my name was turning forty-four
and the building did not from that age go alone
into pieces wheeled away
but all through these years
rubber bands have continued to come to me
sometimes many together
arriving to accompany me although
the whole country has changed
means of travel accelerated

signs almost totally replaced traffic re-routed every
love altered
the stamps re-issued and
smells of streets and apples
moved on

the stone city in
the river has changed and of course
the river
and all words even those unread in
envelopes
all those shining cars vanished
after them entire roads gone like kite strings
incalculable records' print grown finer
just the names at that followed by smoke of numbers
and high buildings turned to glass in
other air oh one clear day

I am a different
foot of a same person in the same river
yet rubber bands lead to me and
from me across great distances
I do not recognize them coming nor remember them going
and still they continue to find me and pass like starlight

St. Vincent's

Thinking of rain clouds that rose over the city
on the first day of the year

in the same month
I consider that I have lived daily and with
eyes open and ears to hear
these years across from St. Vincent's Hospital
above whose roof those clouds rose

its bricks by day a French red under
cross facing south
blown-up neo-classic façades the tall
dark openings between columns at
the dawn of history
exploded into many windows
in a mortised face

inside it the ambulances have unloaded
after sirens' howling nearer through traffic on
Seventh Avenue long
ago I learned not to hear them
even when the sirens stop

they turn to back in
few passers-by stay to look
and neither do I

at night two long blue
windows and one short one on the top floor
burn all night
many nights when most of the others are out
on what floor do they have
anything

I have seen the building drift moonlit through geraniums
late at night when trucks were few
moon just past the full
upper windows parts of the sky
as long as I looked
I watched it at Christmas and New Year
early in the morning I have seen the nurses ray out through
arterial streets
in the evening have noticed interns blocks away
on doorsteps one foot in the door

I have come upon the men in gloves taking out
the garbage at all hours
piling up mountains of
plastic bags white strata with green intermingled and
black
I have seen one pile
catch fire and studied the cloud
at the ends of the jets of the hoses
the fire engines as near as that
red beacons and
machine-throb heard by the whole body
I have noticed molded containers stacked outside
a delivery entrance on Twelfth Street
whether meals from a meal factory made up with those
mummified for long journeys by plane
or specimens for laboratory
examination sealed at the prescribed temperatures
either way closed delivery

and approached faces staring from above
crutches or tubular clamps
out for tentative walks
have paused for turtling wheelchairs
heard visitors talking in wind on each corner
while the lights changed and
hot dogs were handed over at the curb
in the middle of afternoon
mustard ketchup onions and relish
and police smelling of ether and laundry
were going back

and I have known them all less than the papers of our days
smoke rises from the chimneys do they have an incinerator
what for
how warm do they believe they have to maintain the air
in there

several of the windows appear
to be made of tin
but it may be the light reflected
I have imagined bees coming and going
on those sills though I have never seen them

who was St. Vincent

The Shuttles

Remembering glitter on the first river
I begin to imagine the chances against
any fabric ever occurring
threads at last becoming original torn cloth
night numberless with lights
flying apart in galaxies I reach out
to imagine becoming one anything
once
among the chances in the rare
aging fabric happening
all the way for the first time

III

The Vineyard

– for Bill Matthews

Going up through the hill called the vineyard
that seems nothing but stone
you come to a tangle of wild plum and hazel bushes
the spring in the cliff like the sex of a green woman
and the taste of the water
and of the stone

you come to the fox's cave in the yellow clay
under the foot of the stone
and barely out of reach lime-crusted nests
of swallows
and in the cliff higher up
holes of swifts and bees
solitary grass

all that stone faces southward
and a little to the east
full of crevices
bats and small birds
foxes and wild honey
clear to the top they call it
the vineyard
where earliest the light
is seen that bids the cock crow

Crossing Place

I crossed the stream
on the rocks
in the summer
evening

trying not to spill
the pitcher of water
from the falls

Summer Night on the Stone Barrens

In the first hours of darkness
while the wide stones are still warm from the sun
through the hush waiting for thunder
a body falls out of a tree
rat or other soft skin
one beat of one heart on the bare stone
gets up and runs on
lightning flaps on the lifted horizon
both scattered beyond black leaves
nearby different cricket notes
climb and the owl cries
the worn moon will rise late among clouds
unseen larks rang at sunset
over yellow thistles of that day
I am under the ancient roof alone
the beams are held up by forgotten builders
of whom there were never pictures
I love voices not heard
but I love them
from some of them with every breath
I go farther away
and to some I return even through storm and sleep
the stillness is a black pearl
and I can see into it while the animals fall
one at a time at immeasurable intervals

September Plowing

For seasons the walled meadow
south of the house built of its stone
grows up in shepherd's purse and thistles
the weeds share April as a secret
finches disguised as summer earth
click the drying seeds
mice run over rags of parchment in August
the hare keeps looking up remembering
a hidden joy fills the songs of the cicadas

two days' rain wakes the green in the pastures
crows agree and hawks shriek with naked voices
on all sides the dark oak woods leap up and shine
the long stony meadow is plowed at last and lies
all day bare
I consider life after life as treasures
oh it is the autumn light

that brings everything back in one hand
the light again of beginnings
the amber appearing as amber

Working into Autumn

Daylight clears after rain to show cool morning
pools in the stones echo birds' water-songs
new growth is washed on tall trees before the leaves turn
hens stray across empty pastures jays ignore them
gliding over them onto the glittering grass laughing
yesterday toward sunset horizon clouds parted
and mosquitoes sailed in glass rain by the open window
where I remained the distance came to me
all day I caulk a house to launch it at nightfall

Memory of Summer Facing West

Sheep and rocks drifting together before sunset
late birds rowing home across bright spaces
shadows stroking the long day above the earth
wild voices high and far-carrying
at sun's descent toward ripening grain

The Love for October

A child looking at ruins grows younger
but cold
and wants to wake to a new name
I have been younger in October
than in all the months of spring
walnut and may leaves the color
of shoulders at the end of summer
a month that has been to the mountain
and become light there
the long grass lies pointing uphill
even in death for a reason
that none of us knows
and the wren laughs in the early shade now
come again shining glance in your good time
naked air late morning
my love is for lightness
of touch foot feather
the day is yet one more yellow leaf
and without turning I kiss the light
by an old well on the last of the month
gathering wild rose hips
in the sun

Autumn Evening

In the late day shining cobwebs trailed from my fingers
I could not see the far ends somewhere to the south
gold light hung for a long time in the wild clematis
called old man's beard along the warm wall
now smoke from my fire drifts across the red sun setting
half the bronze leaves still hold to the walnut trees
marjoram joy of the mountains flowers again
even in the light frosts of these nights
and there are mushrooms though the moon is new
and though shadows whiten on the grass before morning
and cowbells sound in the dusk from winter pastures

Kore

α   I have watched your smile in your sleep
     and I know it is the boat
     in which my sun rides under the earth
     all night on the wave of your breath
     no wonder the days grow short
     and waking without you
     is the beginning of winter

β   How is it that I can hear your bird voice now
     trickling among the ice towers
     through the days of the anvil
     as the year turns I carry an echo
     over my own stones and I listen
     my eyes are open looking ahead
     I walk a little ahead of myself touching
     the light air where nobody sees you
     and the sun as it sets through the forest of windows
     unrolls slowly its
     unrepeatable secret
     all the colors of autumn without the leaves

γ   You were shaking and an air full of leaves
flowed out of the dark falls of your hair
down over the rapids of your knees
until I touched you and you grew quiet
and raised to me
your hands and your eyes and showed me
twice my face burning in amber

δ   Already on the first hill with you beside me
at the foot of the ruins I saw through the day
and went on without pausing
loving the unheld air
as a wing might love it flying
toward you unknowing
knowing

ε   Face that I loved when I was a child
nobody in that age believed us
when we said we would go away together
not even when we said that the flood
was on its way
and nobody will find us when it is over

ζ   You slept all the way to the garden
face in the boat of my hand
and we came more than a century late
to the closed gate
and the song the laurel remembers in the dark
the night flute always beginning again
on the untrodden slope
and where we walked in the streets then there was new wine
announced with green boughs over doorways
in the time of the statues

η   Climbing at noon by roofless columns
with the day white on the sea
I did not know the word for the hour
nor for the hunger
nor for your hand
which I was not touching
but could feel in the air
The beginning
comes from before
when the words for it were pictures of strangers
it comes on wings that never waited for their names

θ   In the house at the end of a day of rain the old man
began to recite a poem
no one remembered but everyone wanted to
only before he had finished it he lay down
taking the rest of it with him to sleep
then in the next light after my night's journey
you were running in leaves across a wide street
as I was running
and we had arrived

ι   When they are together our hands are of an age
and a dark light flows up between them
into its feathers
We have brought
nothing with us
but what has come of itself
we pass the stone fragments
the ancient smiles holding out
no hands
like the trees their sisters born older

κ   Autumn is one of the four elements
the air has four seasons strung
to its instrument

each with its own wind
but one note under them   Full moon   The year
has turned in the leafless veins
and the poles of the earth have sounded
I wake looking east hearing
the snow fall and your
feet far from here bare
climbing an untold stair
Long before sunrise hands of a child carrying grapes

λ   At the top of the veins I hear
the finger on the bowstring
I hear my feet continuing
upward I hear you
hair in wind
I learn from you of the bare slope
where you are nowhere in sight
so we climb the mountain together after all
even with it between us

μ   The candles flutter on the stairs of your voice
gold in the dark
and for this
far time you laughed through your whole childhood
and all those years my beloved spiders
guarded the treasure under my house
unlit until the night before you appeared

ν   I have loved you in the four capitals
of four worlds before this one
with its glass season
and the nakedness of their light
wakes me now
and the burning that the year comes back for
leaping the falls of its own
changes

ξ   The sun yellows pages of print
a snow of bats swirls in the streets
distractions
what I thought I knew falls aside a thought at a time
until I see you naked
in your eyes the bronze ferns older than seeing
unfurling above the dark springs

o   In winter far from you
at the thought of your skin
leaves
yet to be
stir in the sleep of roots
the tree
of veins trembles
at a distance and begins
gathering in secret the sibyl's rustling

π   I trust neither memory nor expectation
but even the white days of cities
belong to what they do not see
even the heart of the doubters' light is gold
even when you are not with me
in the flowerless month of the door god
you look at me with your eyes of arrival

ρ   I found you the bracelets of plaited straw
you found me the old tools
that I had been looking for
you knew where they were
in my garden
few are the words for finding
as I told you under the beating flights
of autumn
and will tell you again
as I find them

σ   We came to the red stone
     that they call black in that country
     because it fell out of the night
     before anyone was there
     and it floated ahead of us on the earth
     alone without a shadow
     but the night had not forgotten it
     and its memory even then was falling after it
     out of the future
     past us into that day

τ   Morning to morning
     the same door opening inward
     from both sides
     laugh close as you are
     it is cold in the house
     and I burned up all the matches in the night
     to look at you

υ   Wire trees
     days with telephones
     pronouncing into black lamps
     trying to get them to light
     rubbing them
     you appear in a gray street
     having heard nothing
     expecting nothing
     with the light behind you
     and our shadows burn the buildings

φ   Thirty days after the solstice
     forms of ripe wheat
     emerge from the tips of the branches
     Far outside them
     here
     where you have never been

I reach for you with my eyes
I call you with my body
that knows your one name

χ   Days when I do not hear you
it seems that the season flows backward
but it is only
I
of hollow streets
deaf smoke
rain on water

ψ   We cross the smooth night lake together
in the waiting boat
we are welcomed without lights
again and again we emerge by day
hand in hand
from all four corridors at once
under the echoing dome
guided by what has not been said

ω   The shadow of my moving foot
feels your direction
you come toward me
bringing the gold through the rust
you step to me through the city of amber
under the moon and the sun
voice not yet in the words
what is spoken is already
another year

Passage

In autumn in this same life
I was leaving a capital
where an old animal
captured in its youth
one that in the wild
would never have reached such an age
was watching the sun set
over nameless
unapproachable trees
and it is spring

In the Pass

Eleven horsemen gather at the hollow bridge
the light is cold and a snowy wind is blowing
the waterfall crashes and the stream below it
is bounding over the rocks under the ice
white spray has crusted on the planks
each of the horsemen as he rounds the cliff
and the bridge comes in sight
thinks of a bird and a woman
and dismounts and leads his horse over
into the spring and the blossoming valley
they are all the same horseman
falcon
mango-daughter

Spring Equinox Full Moon

I breathe to you
love in the south in the many
months of spring

hibiscus in dark hair water
at the source
shadows glistening to hips
thighs slender sunset shining shores

fingers rolled fragrant leaves
presence of deep woods
earth veiled in green drift
that hides running
of small airs
untraceable fine sounds
passing as on a face
feet first drops of rain on a mountain
hands greeting flowers
holding stolen flowers

closed eyes of every creature
sepia and amber days
back
of tall tree
arms' glide
voice of rain forests
birds in tree heights
throat of palm

wrist of palm
palm of palm
fruit nakedness
morsel breasts
melon navel waist of high waterfall
surf laughter face hearing music
body of flight
secret
beach

away from you on a corner of the earth
I want to think for six hours of your hair
which is the invention of singing
daughter of islands
born in the flood of the fish harvest
I see long mornings
lying on your hair
I remember looking for you

The Morning

The first morning
I woke in surprise to your body
for I had been dreaming it
as I do

all around us white petals had never slept
leaves touched the early light
your breath warm as your skin on my neck
your eyes opening

smell of dew

Summer Doorway

I come down from the gold mountains
each of them the light of many years
high up the soughing of cold pines among stones
the whole way home dry grass seething
to these sounds I think of you already there
in the house all my steps lead to

you have the table set to surprise me
you are lighting the two candles

I come to the door quickly to surprise you
but you laugh we laugh you run toward me
under the long skirt your feet are bare
I drop to my knees in the doorway and catch you
holding the backs of your thighs I watch the candle flames
over my head you watch the birds flying home from the sea

The Hosts

You asked what
were the names of those two
old people who lived under the big tree
and gods in disguise visited them though they were poor

they offered the best they had to eat
and opened the oldest wine in the house
the gods went on pouring out pouring out wine
and then promised that it would flow till the ends of their lives

when the shining guests were out of sight he turned to her
by the table and said
this bottle has been in the cave all the time
we have been together

Islands

Wherever I look you are islands
a constellation of flowers breathing on the sea
deep-forested islands mountainous and fragrant
fires on a bright ocean
at the root one fire

all my life I have wanted to touch your ankle
running down to its shore

I beach myself on you
I listen
I see you among still leaves
regard of rock pool
by sun and moon and stars

island waterfalls and their echoes
are your voice your shoulders the whole of you standing
and you turn to me as though your feet were in mist
flowers birds same colors
as your breath
the flowers deliberately smell of you
and the birds make their feathers
not to fly but to
feel of you

Mountain Day

With one dear friend we go up the highest mountain
thousands of feet into the birdless snow
and listen to our breaths in the still air
for a long time beside the observatories
later we stretch out on the dark crumbled
lava slope looking
west at the sun yellowing the clouds below
then go down past the wild cows to the cabin
getting there just before sunset
and eat by the fire laughing at what we have
forgotten to bring
afterward we come out and lie
braided together looking up
at Cassiopeia over the foothill

Snowline

Turning climbing slowly in late spring among
black trunks of high pines
talking of our lives few white words flying
up into fringed boughs
unexpectedly we catch sight
across an immeasurable valley
of the long peak capped with snow and slanting light
that we saw far above us at morning
now appears scarcely higher than we are
cloud-cliff of moonlight by day
standing still we feel we could touch it
days distant in gleaming air
then we see footsteps of snow climbing all around us
into white sky

Twilight

Oh you are never tame
fire on a mountain
eyes beside water
first day of petals

lying across the bed
in afternoon rainlight
arms of evening
wherever we are is a shore

Late Snow

Wallflowers leaping on slope facing southeast
steep waves glittering
three weeks in spring mountain winds

sweetvetch beardtongue bluebells
skyflowers
thimbleberry blossoming like a rose
white of catching all near sunlight
cold rain two days on long sparse mountain grass
darkening lichened boulders under pine trees
once we wake and it has snowed everywhere
from the railing you wave your arms to the pines
they are holding white sky above white ground
their own feet still sleeping in dark forest
birds shaking few pieces of day from boughs
in white cloud hushed light through canyon
feather sounds
snow falls into your dark hair

June Rain

The rain of the white valley the clear rain
the rain holding the whole valley while it falls
the mountain rain the high rain onto the mountain
as it rained on the mountain on the night we met
the many days' rain shadowless rain
blowing from the long eaves to go on falling
the rain whose ancestors
with no names
made the valley
the nameless shining rain whose past lives
made all the valleys
the author of the rivers
with unchanged and final voice
the rain that falls in the new open streams
running down the dirt roads on the mountain
the rain falling hour after hour into summer
the unexpected rain the long surprise
the rain we both watch at the same window

the rain we lie and listen to together
the rain we hear returning through the night
the rain we do not hear
the open rain

White Summer Flower

Nameless

white poppy
whoever looks at you is alone

when I look at your petals
each time they open

and think of each time
that I have passed them

I know that I have wanted
to say Wait

and why should they

Trees

I am looking at trees
they may be one of the things I will miss
most from the earth
though many of the ones that I have seen
already I cannot remember
and though I seldom embrace the ones I see
and have never been able to speak
with one
I listen to them tenderly

their names have never touched them
they have stood round my sleep
and when it was forbidden to climb them
they have carried me in their branches

Grass Beginning July

A pause at the top of a leap
a pause in the sun
itself as we say
east wind drifts up the steep hillside
on the mountain the heat of noon
has dried the full-grown
manes of the grass
the late-running herds
they run among the yucca
the deer-browsed yucca
yellow daisies cactus flowers
they run past rocks waiting on the slope
and prayer flag clothes drying
on the way to the trees
all of us moving together

IV

The Coin

I have been to a fair alone
and across the river from the tented marketplace
and the church
were the green sagging balconies from which
during the occupation
the bodies of many
of the men of the town
hung for days in full view
of the women who had been their wives
I watched men in long
black coats selling animals
I watched money going
to a fat woman in white
who held pieces of white cheese
wrapped in white paper
out into the sunlight
I watched an old woman selling cut flowers
counting change
I looked at her teeth and lips
the dark kerchief on her head
there were carnations and
summer flowers rolled in wet newspaper
I considered the wares of a man
with a pile of whetstones
I watched three turtledoves eating in a cage
one of them white
one of them dyed pink
one pale blue
a coin in with their grain
pigeons watching from
the church windowsills
others flying overhead
some few bright clouds moving
all of it returns without a sound

Ferry Port

We will be leaving now in less than a week
meanwhile we are
staying in a house in the port
helpful friends
have found us a top floor with a round balcony
like the plank roof of a tower
jutting over the corner of the back street
we sit out in the late afternoon
long grass and the trees of a park
on the far side
and a few cars on the hill
I try to imagine what it would be like
to live here
say for a winter
we go almost every day
to the library
and read about the island we are leaving
we walk around the harbor
the ferry building is the largest in town
new behind high wire fences
yellow tiles five storys
blocking out the view of the harbor entrance
much larger and more solid
than the creaking wooden
sun-beamed ferry barns of my childhood
now removed
this one is like a government
which employs everyone
our car is ready to be loaded
we have scarcely unpacked
it will be strange to be on the mainland
as it is to be on the earth itself
we drove to the port on a Friday
we are to sail on a Saturday

the fat woman shorter than we are
whose house we are in
will stand in her red dress
with her arms around us
in the evening
under the girders in the smell of oil in the wind
asking us questions
and telling us that we have been here
a week and a day

The Banquet

Travelling north day after day
your eyes darken
and the roads become guides knowing
a further evening

white sky later and later
and one by one
houses with blue ceilings
painted every year
doors and windows from a childhood
that was yours
shrink
seen again years afterward
for one moment late in the day
when there is no time

in that age you went home from school
to the room where the crystals
are lit now for the banqueters
raising their glasses

hours before the first star

Service

You can see that
nobody lives in
castles like that
any more
thank God I suppose
and the castle gatehouse
has been turned
into a gas station
which is closed because
nobody comes to that
back street on a Sunday
a dog is tied to the front door
in the rain
all afternoon
trained to bark at footsteps
but not cars
the wet yellow roses sag
in the empty green
shadow-bricked gardens
white
curtains are drawn
on all the bay windows

Some of the Masts

I hear my feet resound on a wharf
echoed from other wharves
through the centuries
the fishing boats are all moored
in the evening
unlit against harbor dusk
the hulls darker already than the gray
photographs of them

ladders folded against
tall cranes for unloading
nets dangling from long hooks
no glitter from gulls' eyes
whirlpools of rope almost full
small waves rocking under the wharf
as I go on around the harbor
by daybreak they will all be at sea

North Wind

In summer
come the old dreams of living on a boat
and walking home to it as the evening
is beginning
along a dry wagon road
bordered with poplars
between ripening fields
long ago
arm around a soft woman
and the dreams of upland stone houses
quaking at hand in cicada sound
and those of a cabin farther in the woods
with the forester's whole family for guides
and coming to hear a rushing stream
and the old man saying
Get down it's the north wind
and all of us lying down in the woods
for a while
thinking of the green cabin
that needs paint
but still has all the old furniture

Island

After two years
we rowed to the island
before it got dark
some were still swimming
in the short summer
on the sand behind us
though the sun
had gone
the sound of far
splashing
carried over the quiet water
through the dripping
of the oars
on the island there was no one
only trees and
open twilit grass under them
no wind
birds already sleeping
but no stars no cloud
almost on the horizon
against a low line of evergreens
a cabin steamer passing
slowly between lakes
with its lights on
then as we were coming back
clear sky
long blue star falling

Junction

Far north a crossroad in mud
new cement curbs a few yards each way
rain all day

two men in rubber boots
hurry along under one plastic
carrying loud radio playing music
pass tin shack surrounded by
broken windshields
paintings of north places
only hotel
has no name
no light to its sign
river from bridge long misted mirror
far houses and red boats float
above themselves in gray sky
martins were hunting
in the morning
over logjams by another shore
cold suppertime
thinking of hares in boggy woods
and footprints of clear water

Remembering a Boatman

After sundown yellow sky beyond shadow mountains
range upon range in long twilight under few distant clouds
darkening pastures run into the bays
birds are already asleep high on the unlit roan cliffs
straw light still flickers on the water
between two headlands in short summer
at last a long boat rowed by one man standing
appears slowly from behind a headland on the right
and starts across
too far away to hear the sounds of the wood
or see colors
a few times the wake turns up light
then I forget him for years

Assembly

Nomads gather in autumn
driving herds to the great auctions
of animals on the gold earth
by then there is blood in the trees
nights are already cold
daybreak white
some of them open stalls by the river
and hang up for sale
loose pelts of different animals
and fur garments stitched with sinews
at moments during the summer
in upland pastures among birds
some play instruments
others sing clapping their hands

Old Garden

One year I seem to have started north many times
standing in a garden
looking at a mountain
over a wall
once I went to the sea and watched the red sun
rise from its peak
watched it set white in the sea veil
as the moon came up
nights I walked on wet sand
and swam looking up
days in palm leaf shadows
I listened
I came to a dry river
in late afternoon one time
place that I thought I knew
and found among stream-bed stones

one white clay dove
in some way broken
there was my father
I came to a full river
another time
between low shores at dusk
and as I crossed over
one bird flew calling
so that I could hear
but not words
that may have been my mother
that year
and one time I woke every morning on a hill
and wanted to remain there
on the way north through the mountains

The Fig Tree

Against the south wall of a monastery
where it catches the first sun
a fig tree a shadowy fig tree
stands by the door
all around the flowing trunk
suckers grow
it is against
the law of the church to pull them out
nobody remembers why
tree roots older than the monastery

The Windows

Here is a child who presses his head to the ground
his eyes are open
he sees through one window

the flat gray ocean
upside down
with an arbor of islands hanging from it
all the way to the horizon
and he himself is hanging from nothing
he might step down
and walk on the old sky far down there
out to the clouds
in the far islands
he might step on the clouds where they have worn shiny
he might jump from cloud to cloud
he watches lights flash
on and off along the dark shores
and the lights moving among the overhead islands
he feels his head like a boat on a beach
he hears the waves break around his ears
he stands up and listens
he turns to a room full of his elders
and the lights on
blue day in the far empty windows
and without moving he flies

The Falcons

There were years when I knew
the flowers in the red stone walls

now in the courtyard where I have returned with you
we drink the wine of visitors
the temperature of the cellars

dusk is welling
out of the dried blood of the masonry
no hour remains on the sundial
by now the owls of the tower corners

are waking on their keepers' fists
but it is still day
out in the air
and three falcons appear there
over the courtyard

no feathers on heads or breasts
and they fly down to us
to our wrists and between them
then hover and perch just above us
keeping us in sight
waiting
they are waiting for us

this time they will come with us
when we leave the island
tonight for the rest of our lives

The Trestle

A postcard held
by one white thumbtack
to the tan wallpaper
above my head
in a room I stood in as a child
showed in brown the view
once long ago from this
tall train bridge
trembling over the gorge
with the tracks far below there
where we have just been
by the glittering rapids
under the black trees
past the only inn
we see it from here

as it is now
painted
between the moving girders

Talk of Fortune

I meet her on the street
she says she is away a lot but it was
actually when she was living here
she came home to the apartment house
which I have just left
and inside by the mailboxes
she found a small old
woman who seemed to be trying
to open the inside door
and looked as though she had been
crying or it could have been laughing
and they tried to talk but
the old woman could not
speak more than a few words
and yet she was well dressed
even old velvet
and when the door was opened for her
she would not go in
for anything
but kept smiling and asking for
something or somebody in
another language
and when she could not make herself
understood she gave
my friend a leaf and went
away and the next day
my friend found a lot of money

The Fountain

An old woman from the country
who sells tickets for sex shows
and looks at the buyers' faces
gave a party
in her kitchen
for her family and their friends
many of whom she did not even know
and she served everybody
yellow cake and meringues
made from her own eggs
as she told the company more than once
and no bag feed she said
she fed them on
oh yes you do grandma
said the small boy whose bed was in the corner
look she said and opened the back door
to show the hens in the evening light
scratching around the fountain

Sun

Dark rain at
winter solstice
and in the morning

rosemary under clear sky
bird on south doorstep
poised like a stone

The Flight

— for Bruce and Fox McGrew

At times in the day
I thought of a fire to watch
not that my hands were cold
but to have that doorway to see through
into the first thing
even our names are made of fire
and we feed on night
walking I thought of a fire
turning around I caught sight of it
in an opening in the wall
in another house and another
before and after
in house after house that was mine to see
the same fire the perpetual bird

FEATHERS FROM THE HILL

(1978)

Time of Tree Cutting

Cold August
mice roll
empty nutshells

———

Darkness that covers
and uncovers the moon
shadow of a wing

———

Waking
hanging upward into the rushing summer
calling

———

Everything is
the answer
too fast

———

Where the cliff
splits
later the dove nests

———

Stony slopes buckwheat smell
wings of landing plover
shiver

———

Nearby one monkey at sunset
ate in silence
watching the lightning

———

The colors look back at the trees
but the birds shut their eyes
thinking to see it all again

———

Along the white hill
owl floats
weighed down with moonlight

———

Nobody knows who lived here
the roof is gone
the eastern cloud swallows the stars

———

Sunlit woods
feather falls
everywhere ready for it

———

Laughter of crows late in the month
spun saucer settling
sunset moving south

Summer Canyon

Some of the mayflies
drift on into June
without their names

———

Spring reappears in the evening
oyster cloud sky catches in pines
water light wells out of needles after sundown

———

On small summit pine hollow
field chickweed under trees
split white petals drifting over shadows

—————

Two crows call to each other
flying over
same places

—————

In high mountains
the late grass
grows as fast as it can

—————

Because of things not even remembered
we are here
listening to the water

—————

Three broad blue petals
I do not know
what kind of flower

—————

Among the pines above me
flowers from days ago
are about to open

—————

Leaves never seen before
look how they have grown
since we came here

—————

After midnight wind drops
belled cat walks the hillside
under black trees

———

Day's end green summer stillness
pine shadows drift far out
on long boards

———

Mourning dove sound
cricket sound
no third

———

Afternoon breeze prowls
with a tail
through tall green upland grass

———

Half moon light midsummer
unseen pheasant among bright rocks
echoes its own voice

———

All day the wind blows
and the rock
keeps its place

———

A silence begins
soon many feet
are heard running

———

Black tree trunks in shade
outside a house
with wooden floors

———

Birds on the roof
if I went up to see
they would be gone

———

For each voiceless flower
there is a voice among
the absent flowers

———

Far away a dog barks
on a windy hilltop
beyond which the sun is setting

———

Sunlight after rain
reflections of ruffled water
cross the ceiling

———

High in the east full moon
and far below on the plain
low clouds and lightning

———

Birds hidden
in moonlit boughs
call from dreams

———

Hot wind at noon
pine cones from dying tree
fall full of seeds

———

Early dusk
pine needles already shining
before rain

———

Line of smoke
writes on
sunlight

———

Flecks of bright down
sail up the day
clear out of the canyon

———

Mountain of
butterflies
hurries

———

Whistle of
mourning dove's wings
stretches the shadows

———

Early I saw
where the sun comes from
here

———

Under a pine at noon
I listen to plates
clattering in a kitchen

———

At the same time every day
clouds come over the mountain
what was I thinking when they appeared

———

Jay clatters through dark pines
it remembers
something it wants there among them

———

Tree toads tighten their notes
numberless yellow daisies
rise through gray grass

———

Sudden rain
army of light passes
with dark footprints

———

Lizard grows up
to be gray twig
in summer

———

Opening my eyes I see
burning alone in blue
the morning star

———

Solitary wasp writes
white eggs
up south window

———

Thistledown
already far from its flower
and still snow on the peaks

———

Young deer standing in headlights
in ditch below cliff
cars coming both ways

———

South slope running to seed
chipmunk squeak shadows
crickets trill long dry grass

———

Even among spoons
favorites emerge
days rising through water

———

Gray voice
nuthatch after sunset
nothing to call it

———

No earlier
could anything that is here
have been

———

A thistledown
is the moon for a moment
then thistledown again

———

Lizard rainwalk on bright boards
rain stops and looks out
washed air

———

Moth studies bark
not moving while
daylight lasts

———

For an age lizards run on gray places
and grown beetles set out from pines
in the heat

———

Too late the chain saws
scream into echoing trunks
finding corridors empty

———

Gray rocks darken
wet bronze pine bark echoes jay shriek
across tall rainy yellow grass

———

Jay calls at night and wakes
flying through dark branches
faster than it can see

———

Pine needles many as stars
one word for all the trees ever seen
and their lifetimes

————

Yellow clothesline empty
raw pole in woods
rain drips from clothespins

————

One night for a moment
beautiful animal
never seen before

————

With lengthening summer
the wild dove's flight
grows louder

————

Steep yellow grass rain
transparent everything I remember
other lives

————

August midnight
horse snorts
in cricket dark

————

Garbage dog bell cat
kitchen mouse banister jay
ceiling chipmunk

————

Afternoon sun wet boughs
smell of autumn in August
schoolbell anvil echoes in empty woods

———

Pines against sky of mist
where I am now
in a breath of a mountain

———

Night of rain onto late summer
cool morning again
cloud canyon

Sound of Rapids of Laramie River in Late August

White flowers among white stones
under white windy aspens
after night of moonlight and thoughts of snow

Fireweed

One morning the days have grown shorter
and fireweed is purple
on the mountains

———

Yellow-winged
grasshoppers clatter through high
windy valley

———

Sound of rain on tent
light from wet sagebrush
on all sides

———

Sundown across shallow stream
magpies bathe together
in aspen thicket

———

After rain cold evening
gray clouds dark south gorge
smell of more rain coming

———

Horses and trees move
in same waves cool night
summer really gone

———

Breasts of swallows turning
flash in morning
among their voices

———

Meadow of sagebrush in flower
cat sits in the middle
fur of morning sunlight

———

Sound of tires on cobbles
decades ago
roars past me now with no car

———

Afternoon moves through
empty tent
cushion at foot of pole

———

Human shadows
walk on tent wall
inside and outside

———

Old woman young woman
baby in green knapsack shouting
past tree after tree

———

Afternoon breeze comes down valley
following small stream
and finds horses

———

Knothole looks out
through a branch
that has come and gone

———

Flies convene
in a patch of sunlight
a day on a calendar

———

Same gong
each hand strikes
different note

———

I leave the tent breathing
without dreams
and walk out on my own

———

Child holds hourglass
above his head
and looks up

———

Last day of August
western bluebirds in
pine shadow

———

In full day
tent pole passes through
big star

———

A moment at a time
the mountain rises
out of empty sky

In the Red Mountains

Blue chairs hang empty
waiting in clear
September sky

———

Daybreak mist in valley
skylark rises
through green floor of cloud

———

Light evening rain
eleven magpies
dance in twilight

Yellow light
memory in aspens
of first frost

Chain saw three minutes
hours later in rain
smell of resin

Wrinkled mountains
end of autumn day
peach down

The colors move
but not
the evening clouds

Moth shadow circles floor
moth alights
by my foot

Through black pines
colors on the mountain
climb down the days

On summits last year's snow
gray with waiting
clear sky white clouds of autumn

―――

Slow bee
still searching yellow day
before frost

―――

Leaves begin to fall
old road appears on the mountains
never anyone's

―――

Hawk flake turns
slowly above ridges
in far blue eye

―――

Aspen glare
migrant blackbirds'
reed-voices

―――

Gold trees
turn into
smoke again

―――

At last
leaves fall
from bare sky

―――

Leaves still on branches
turn at night into
first snow

———

Many times clouds were mountains
then one morning mountains
woke as clouds

———

Feet in mist
feel the earth move
from under

———

After sunrise
autumn mists part
showing another valley

———

Two snows come and gone
brown cows' valley pastures
gray undersides of olive leaves

———

I see my parents
through a grove of white trees
on a day of winter sunlight

———

Shadow ravine
snow blue as smoke full of sunlight
over black fire

———

Wakes of light
ray out on dark pond
where ducks swim before winter

——

Snow blows from the roof
the whole room
flies out over the white valley

Road

In early snow
going to see a friend
I pass thousands of miles of fences

Island City

Green corn stalks rustle
beginning to dry
on a hill above the sea

——

Pile of box houses
with wires on every side
and box voices and box dogs

——

Around a corner
somebody who's a city
pounds all day on a tin door

——

Only two houses away
a neighbor
is a piano playing

——

A breeze through the house
and one fly rushes
from window to window

———

Morning noon and evening
the old woman turns on the sprinkler
and watches

———

The landlord's children
lock up their dog
and shout at it

———

Living it up
in the afternoon
at the shopping center

———

Under the traffic light
silent paper boy
watches the cars

———

Whole crowd nosing
for shade for the baby
while they go fishing

———

Backs in a row at the sea's edge
bow late in the day
hooking tiny fish

———

Little girl's belly
old man's belly
a sail on the horizon

———

Old dog under a bush
head on his paws
watches waves climb the sand

———

All the guests in the neighbor's garden
ask where the neighbors will go
now he's retiring

———

Toward the sea
wings of flies flash
with sunset

———

Suddenly wrinkles appear
on the water
and then are gone again

———

Going away over water
a cloud
from a cloud

———

So many lives in the evening
staring at the one
program

———

When his television
is off
the neighbor can't stop coughing

———

As I grow older
the cities spread
over the earth

———

A tree stirs
and the curtain
draws back from the window

———

Ward of unlit terraces
the hour of night barks
and echoes

———

At night the autumn mist
arrives and arrives in silence
but the eaves drip through the dark

———

Sound of late tires carries
from an unseen street
through cool leaves

———

It isn't the moon
but the city reflected
from the house fronts on the hill

———

One cricket starts up
in the still moonlight
and wakes the refrigerator

———

Rain from the full moon
all at once washes away
deep dust

———

By the setting moon
a rat runs
on the dry leaves of the woodrose

———

Sleeping I saw the new moon
through the open window
of an unknown kitchen

———

Lizard clacks at daybreak
in the dark of mango trees
when the morning star is alone

———

Packing again
to the sound
of autumn rain

By the Mango Trees

A little higher
the green hill hides
in rain

———

The trees bow with the wind
but the houses
forget

———

Rain on the tin roof
lizard hands on the tin ceiling
listening

———

In the evening sunlight
the hill pasture
is ripening

———

Lizard just hatched
such a hurry
tail gets in front of the head

———

A spider hangs
from a new thread
in the light from the window

———

Lizard runs out on a beam
shits and
looks down

———

White balsam flowers
moons in
full moonlight

———

Late at night
the dogs bark for hours
then the rain comes

———

Great dipper stands
on its handle
leaning against the paling sky

———

When the rooster crows
a rat shakes
the orange tree

———

Old dry banana leaf
one of my aunts
but I can't remember which

———

Loud yellow truck passes
the yellow lilies
in the wind

———

Living at the farm
she airs her baby
up and down the road

———

How time disappears
while we live under
the big tree

Warm Pastures

Half the night sky deep cloud
and rain falls
through moonlight

——

Moonlight before dawn
voices of plovers waking in flight
over foggy pastures

——

Birds' feet
scratch the tin roof
daybreak

——

Lighthouse goes on
flashing flashing
as the sun rises

——

Still not seasoned
rooftree runs through row
of old sparrow nests

——

The first light
is climbing the road
through black trees

——

Hearing rain on big leaves
I look up
and all the white birds have gone

——

Can't see the rain
but see where
the sand jumps

———

Loud rain
fog on the hills
mud from the faucets

———

Week of rain
voice of ground dove
from wet woods

———

As he mends
the wire pasture fence
the waves keep breaking behind him

———

Black cows
by late morning
are the big tree's shadow

———

How far the plover comes
to stand in the grass
by the stairs

———

Peel the round-ended
pineapple fields
off the raw hills

———

Crop-duster pilot goes
home and washes his
hands his hands

———

Christmas Eve bright sunlight
white smoke
smelling of sugar

———

Sun drops into smoke
the cane fields appear
burning

———

In the wild
they know
they are rare

———

In the gold evening
the tall trees are leaning
toward the flying voices

———

Shadow
overflows a spring
down in the pasture

———

Another cloud
at evening passing
the distant island

———

Suddenly the shadows
of the wheeling plovers
go out

———

As the year was ending
I heard a breath
start the tin windmill

———

When the moon sets
the sea slowly
disappears

———

Fond of the clock
because of the hours
it has told

———

In the night grass
cricket is travelling
into one note

———

I wake touching her
and lie still to listen
to the warm night

Sheep Clouds

Wake on the train
and they tell you
what you didn't see

———

In the mist at daybreak
row of socks hanging
over the vegetable garden

———

Once you leave
you have a name
you can't remember

———

Already at the thought
of the late spring
the window is open

———

Mist fades in the sun
sheep lean into the wall
shirt breathes at a window

———

In the spring evening
a crow calls
and I come back from the years

———

The cornflowers
keep painting
the faded air

———

Long twilight
before midsummer
all the clouds are moon

———

Old branch alive alive
moored in the darkening sky
sound of the stream

————

The moth brings
the map
of both sides

————

Just before dawn
the nightingale
starts something new

————

Midsummer stars fade
the oriole echoes
the nightingale

————

When it says
good-bye
say thank you

————

Deep in cloud
a day with summer flowers
and small bells ringing

————

Starts too near
ever to
arrive

————

Late in summer
the birds draw
closer together

———

In a summer of mist
through the evening
a road of mist

———

Hay in and a cow sick
the unwatched television
flickers on his face

———

What is an itch
that nobody should speak
well of it

———

Sun sinks on red pastures
and a dog barks
at the sound of a closing door

———

Oh the sun sets in the oaks
and the white lady
calls to the mice of the fields

———

Stars of August what
are you
doing

———

Moon setting
in the oak tree
wakes one blackbird

———

Bright September
the shadow of the old walnut tree
has no age

———

On the reflections of the freight cars
after the frost
water lilies

OPENING THE HAND

(1983)

I

The Waters

I was the whole summer remembering
more than I knew
as though anything could stand still
in the waters

there were lives that turned and appeared to wait
and I went toward them looking
sounds carry in water but not
what I called so far

sun and moon shone into
the moving water
and after many days
joys and griefs I had not thought were mine

woke in this body's altering dream
knowing where they were
faces that would never die returned
toward our light through mortal waters

The Oars

My father was born   in a house by a river
nobody knows   the color of the water
already seeds had set   in the summer weeds
the house needed paint   but nobody will see

after the century turned   he sat in a rowboat
with its end on the bank   below the house
holding onto the oars   while the trains roared past
until it was time for him   to get up and go

Sunset Water

How white my father looked   in the water
all his life he swam   doggie paddle
holding hurried breaths   steering an embarrassed smile

long after he has gone I rock in smooth waves near the edge of the sea
at the foot of a hill   I never saw before
or so I imagine   as the sun is setting
sharp evening birds   and voices of children
echo each other   across the water

one by one the red waves   out of themselves reach through me

The Waving of a Hand

   First rose a low shore   pastures green to the water
that my father must have seen   but did he know it at the time
and maybe it seemed to him then   that he was arriving
   a few white façades   far off on the land's edge
lighthouse not yet flashing   small coast guard station
all faintly gleaming   under low sky
by the wide river mouth   late in the day
cold wind sweeping   green estuary
but everything still   calm and as it should be
   water sound sliding   close by under wood
everyone lying down   in the thin vessel
except the one sailor   leaning against the mast
face never seen   turned away forward
catching last sunlight   eyes toward the sea
waves out there suddenly blue   and sky darkening
   yet I was standing   in an old wooden house
where surely my father had stood   but had he known it then
I was among friends   he had never met
   out in back through the window   the same quiet yard

and small wooden study   beyond it under trees
it was growing dark in the room   but no one turned a light on
and the next time   I looked through that window
there was nothing to see in the yard   but a cloud
a white cloud   full of moonlight
and I tapped someone's shoulder   and we both stared
    then we talked of other things   I did not stay
soon it was really night   I ate with friends it rained
three times I climbed   a long staircase
the first time and the second   someone was at the top
    hundreds of miles   to the west
my father died   just before one in the morning

Strawberries

    When my father died I saw   a narrow valley

it looked as though it began   across the river
from the landing where he was born   but there was no river

I was hoeing the sand   of a small vegetable plot
for my mother   in deepening twilight
and looked up in time   to see a farm wagon
dry and gray   horse already hidden
and no driver   going into the valley
carrying a casket

                    and another wagon
coming out of the valley   behind a gray horse
with a boy driving   and a high load
of two kinds of berries   one of them strawberries

    that night when I slept   I dreamed of things
wrong in the house   all of them signs
the water of the shower   running brackish

and an insect of a kind   I had seen him kill
climbing around   the walls of his bathroom
    up in the morning   I stopped on the stairs
my mother was awake   already and asked me
if I wanted a shower   before breakfast
and for breakfast she said   we have strawberries

A Pause by the Water

After the days of walking   alone in mountains
between cities and after the nights   again under dripping trees
coming down I kept seeing   in my mind the ocean
though I knew it would not be   like anything I imagined

after hearing of the old man's   dying and after the burial
between rainy morning and rainy evening   the start of a cold
        summer
coming down the misted path alone   I kept finding
in my thought the ocean   though I told myself
step by step that it could never   be at all like that

warm simple and there   full of real day
blue and familiar   as far as the sky
breathing softly   beyond the pines and
the white unprinted   sand and I would
surely not be sailing   in that small boat
like the one I wanted   by a lake long ago

and it is true there is   this wind off the ocean
so that I shiver with   my collar up
standing on the splashed cement   of the sea wall
and through the foggy field glasses   from before the war
I can make out several   channel markers leaning
and a brace of freighters   a tug with brown barges
the faint domes of gas tanks   on the distant shore

if I did not know where I was   I could be anywhere
with that one sail   crossing the lenses
heeled over so that I   can watch the gleam of the hull
white but for one black patch   recurring between waves
as it passes in the cold of my hands   while behind me
I feel the dusk   surfacing on the swimming pool
and from the far end the eyes   of the muffled couple
in deck chairs under the petals   of frosted glass

who have been coming here   every year for years
soon we will eat our fish   in the lighted room
and later they will show me   pictures of children

Son

As the shadow closed   on the face once my father's
three times leaning forward   far off she called
Good night in a whisper   from before I was born
later through the burial   a wren went on singing

then it was that I left   for the coast to live
a single long mountain   close to the shore
from it the sun rose   and everyone there asked me
who I was   I asked them who they were

at that time I found the cave   under the mountain
drawings still on the walls   carved fragments in the dirt
all my days I spent there   groping in the floor
but some who came from nearby   were wrecking the place for a
        game
garbage through holes overhead   broken cars dead animals
in the evenings they rolled huge rocks   down to smash the roof
nothing that I could do   kept them from it for long

the old story   the old story

and in the mornings the cave   full of new daylight

Sun and Rain

Opening the book   at a bright window
above a wide pasture   after five years
I find I am still standing   on a stone bridge
looking down with my mother   at dusk into a river
hearing the current as hers   in her lifetime

now it comes to me   that that was the day
she told me of seeing my father   alive for the last time
and he waved her back from the door   as she was leaving
took her hand   for a while and said
nothing

        at some signal
in a band of sunlight all the black cows   flow down the pasture together
to turn uphill and stand   as the dark rain touches them

The Houses

Up on the mountain where nobody is looking
a man forty years old in a gray felt hat
is trying to light a fire in the springtime

up on the mountain where nobody
except God and the man's son are looking
the father in a white shirt is trying
to get damp sticks to burn in the spring noon

he crumples newspaper from the luggage compartment
of the polished black Plymouth parked under the young leaves
a few feet away in the overgrown wagon track
that he remembers from another year
he is thinking of somewhere else as the match flame blows

he has somewhere else in mind that nobody knows
as the flame climbs into the lines of print and they curl
and set out unseen into the sunlight
he needs more and more paper and more matches
and the wrapping from hot dogs and from buns
gray smoke gets away among the slender trees

it does not occur to the son to wonder
what prompted his father to come up here
suddenly this one morning and bring his son
though the father looks like a stranger on the mountain
breaking sticks and wiping his hand on the paper
as he crumples it and blowing into the flames
but when his father takes him anywhere they are both strangers

and the father has long forgotten that the son
is standing there and he is surprised
when the smoke blows in his face and he turns
and sees parallel with the brim the boy looking at him
having been told that he could not help and to wait there
and since it is a day without precedents the son
hears himself asking the father whether he may
please see what is down the wagon track and he surprises
himself hearing his father say yes but don't go far

and be very careful and come right back
so the son turns to his right and steps over
the gray stones and leaves his father making
a smoky fire on the flat sloping rock
and after a few steps the branches close overhead
he walks in the green day in the smell of thawed earth
and a while farther on he comes to a turn to the right
and the open light of cleared ground falling away
still covered with the dry grass of last year
by a dark empty barn he can see light through

and before the barn on the left a white house
newly painted with wide gray steps leading
up to the gray floor of the porch where the windows
are newly washed and without curtains so that he
can look into the empty rooms and see the doors
standing open and he can look out
through windows on the other side into the sky
while the grass new and old stands deep all around the house
that is bare in readiness for somebody
the wind is louder than in the wood
the grass hissing and the clean panes rattling

he looks at rusted handles beside bushes
and with that thinks of his father and turns back
into the shadowy wagon track and walks
slowly tree by tree stone by stone under
the green tiers of leaves until he comes
to the smell of smoke and then the long pile of stones
before the clearing where his father is bending
over the fire and turns at the son's voice and calls him
a good boy for coming back and asks whether
he's hungry and holds out a paper plate
they stand in the smoke holding plates while the father
asks the blessing and afterward the son tells him

of the white house the new paint the clean windows
into empty rooms and sky and nobody in sight
but his father says there is no such house along there
and he warns the son not to tell stories
but to eat and after a moment the son
surprises them both by insisting that he has
seen it all just as he said and again the father
scolds him this time more severely returning
from somewhere else to take up his sternness
until the son starts to cry and asks him
to come and see for himself after they have eaten

so when the plates have been burned and the fire
put out carefully and the car packed they walk
without a word down the wagon track where the light
seems to have dimmed as though rain might be on its way
and the trees are more remote than the boy
had thought but before long they reach the opening
where the track turns to the right and there is
the glare of the dry grass but no house no barn
and the son repeats I saw them but the father says
I don't want to hear any more about it

in a later year the father takes the boy
taller now and used to walking by himself
to an old farm in the middle of the state
where he busies himself in the small house he has bought
while the son having been told that he cannot help
walks down the lane past the vacant corn crib and barn
past the red shale banks where the lane descends
beside unkempt pastures with their springs and snakes
into the woods and onto a wooden bridge

still on his father's land he watches the dark water
flow out from under low branches and the small fish
flickering in glass over the black bed and as he
turns and climbs the lane on the far side he sees
to his right below him on the edge of the stream
a low house painted yellow with a wide porch
a gun leaning beside the front door and a dog's chain
fastened to the right of the steps but no dog visible

there appears to be no one in the house and the boy goes
on up the lane through the woods and across pastures
and coming back sees that nothing has changed
the gun still by the door the chain in the same place
he watches to see whether anything moves
he listens he stares through the trees wondering
where the dog is and when someone will come home

then he crosses the stream and returns to his father
indoors and in the evening he remembers
to ask who is living in the yellow house
in the woods on the far side of the stream
which he had understood was his father's land
but his father tells him there is no house there

by then they have left the farm and are driving home
and the son tells the father of the gun by the door
the dog's chain by the front steps and the father
says yes that is his land beyond the stream
but there is no building and nobody living there

the boy stops telling what he has seen
and it is a long time before he comes again
to walk down the lane to the woods and cross the bridge
and see on the far side only trees by the stream

then the farm is sold and the woods are cut and the subject
never brought up again but long after the father
is dead the son sees the two houses

Apparitions

Now it happens in these years   at unguarded intervals
with a frequency   never to be numbered
a motif surfacing in some scarcely known   music of my own
each time the beginning and   then broken off

that I will be looking down   not from a window
and once more catch a glimpse   of them hovering
above a whiteness like paper   and much nearer than I would have
        thought
lines of his knuckles   positions of his fingers
shadowy models of the backs   of my father's hands
that always appeared   to be different from my own

whether as to form texture   role or articulation
with a difference I granted them   from their origin
those stub fingers   as his family would term them
broad and unsprung   deflated somewhat and pallid
that I have seen stand forth one by one   obedient as dogs
so the scissors could cut   the flat nails straight across

they that whitened carrying   small piles of papers
and performed pretending   they knew how
posed with tools   held up neckties and waited
gripped their steering wheel   or my arm before striking
furnished him with complaints   concerning their skin and joints
evoked no music ever   had no comeliness
that I could recognize   when I yet supposed
that they were his alone   and were whole
what time they were younger   than mine are

or again the veins will appear   in their risen color
running over the hands   I knew as my mother's
that surprised me by pausing   so close to me
and I wait for the smell   of parsley and almonds
that I never imagined   otherwise than as hers

to float to me from the polished   translucent skin
and the lightness   of the tapering
well-kept and capable   poised small fingers
and from the platinum   wedding-band (with its gleam
of an outer planet)   that I have watched
finger and thumb of the other   hand slowly turn
and turn   while someone's voice was continuing

those hands that were always   on the way back to something
they that were shaken at the sink   and stripped the water
from each other like gloves   and dried swiftly on the dishtowel
flew above typewriter keys   faster than I could watch
faster than words   and without hesitation
appear again   and I am practicing the piano

that I have not touched   for as long as their age
one of them rises to wait   at the corner of the page
and I feel mistakes approach   that I have just learned not to make

but as I recognize   those hands they are gone
and that is what they are   as well as what they became
without belief I still watch them   wave to no one but me
across one last room   and from one receding car
it is six years now   since they touched anything
and whatever they can be said   to have held at all
spreads in widening rings   over the rimless surface

what I see then are these two   hands I remember
that wash my face   and tie my shoestrings
and have both sides   and a day around them
I do not know   how they came to me
they are nobody's children   who do they answer to
nobody told them to bleed   but their scars are my own
nobody but me   knows what they tell me
of flame and honey   and where you are
and the flow of water   the pencil in the air

Birdie

You don't think anything that I know of
but as for me when I think of you
I don't know how many of you there are
and I suppose you thought there was just the one

how many times you may have been born
as my father's other sisters would say
in your bawdy nobody is interested
in things like that in the family

somebody wrote down though that you was
born one time on April 20

1874 so that my grandmother
at that occasion was thirteen and the hardest thing
to believe in that account as I think of it
is that she was ever thirteen years old
the way we grew up to hide things from each other

so she had a little baby at that age

and that was you Birdie that was one of you
did you know
it presents a different picture of my
grandmother from the one I was brought up to

that was the you she had when she was thirteen
which goes a long way to explain
her puritanism and your gypsy earrings
and all the withered children who came after
and their scorn of your bright colors and your loud heart

and maybe even your son who was delicate
and an artist and painted heads of Jesus
on church walls where they crumbled and could not be moved
and your having a good time and dying in Arizona

except that as everybody knew
that you
was nothing but a mistake in
the writing and the real Birdie came along
when Grandma was into her twenties and she
had her firstborn a little baby girl
which explains nothing

puritanism earrings the children who came after
your son the frail artist the crumbling heads of Jesus
the having a good time and dying in Arizona
that was the you I met one morning in summer
whom nobody could explain for you was different

inviting all them so unexpected
and not heard of for so long your own mother
younger brother younger sisters new nephew
to breakfast laughing and waving your hands

with all the rings and them not listening
saying they was in a hurry to drive farther
and see the family and you going on
telling them everything there was to eat

The Burnt Child

Matches among other things that were not allowed
never would be
lying high in a cool blue box
that opened in other hands and there they all were
bodies clean and smooth blue heads white crowns
white sandpaper on the sides of the box scoring
fire after fire gone before

I could hear the scratch and flare
when they were over
and catch the smell of the striking
I knew what the match would feel like
lighting
when I was very young

a fire engine came and parked
in the shadow of the big poplar tree
on Fourth Street one night
keeping its engine running
pumping oxygen to the old woman
in the basement
when she died the red lights went on burning

Yesterday

My friend says I was not a good son
you understand
I say yes I understand

he says I did not go
to see my parents very often you know
and I say yes I know

even when I was living in the same city he says
maybe I would go there once
a month or maybe even less
I say oh yes

he says the last time I went to see my father
I say the last time I saw my father

he says the last time I saw my father
he was asking me about my life
how I was making out and he
went into the next room
to get something to give me

oh I say
feeling again the cold
of my father's hand the last time

he says and my father turned
in the doorway and saw me
look at my wristwatch and he
said you know I would like you to stay
and talk with me

oh yes I say

but if you are busy he said
I don't want you to feel that you
have to
just because I'm here

I say nothing

he says my father
said maybe
you have important work you are doing
or maybe you should be seeing
somebody I don't want to keep you

I look out the window
my friend is older than I am
he says and I told my father it was so
and I got up and left him then
you know

though there was nowhere I had to go
and nothing I had to do

Talking

Whatever I talk about is yesterday
by the time I see anything it is gone
the only way I can see today
is as yesterday

I talk with words I remember
about what has already happened
what I want to talk about is no longer there
it is not there

today I say only what I remember
even when I am speaking of today

nobody else remembers what I remember
not even the same names

I tell parts of a story
that once occurred
and I laugh with surprise at what disappeared
though I remember it so well

After a Storm

When I come back I find
a place that was never there

once I stood where
the poplar as big as the house
shimmered with streetlight and moonlight
years before
outside the window
by my bed in the first room
and there is no tree there
and the house has no door

again amazed to be alone so young
one time in the country I climbed a hill
to see the night pasture
in the afternoon in spring
and the hollow and deep woods
beyond the bright grass

lying on the white boards
of the leaky boat
that I had dragged up from the lake bottom
after lifting the stones out
and then dried in the sun
and caulked and tarred
and found a mast for in spring

I went on looking up
at the sky above the mast
no breath of wind no cloud
lake water lapping the painted chamber

not even the last to go
are water sounds
wild brooks in the woods
clear streams full of beings
unknown flowers
the doors of water
are not even the last to close
the bells of water not yet the last bells

there are the doors of no water
the bells of no water
the bells of air
if I could take one voice
with me it would be
the sound I hear every day

The Cart

One morning in summer
music flew up out of New
York Avenue
under the bay window

down there a small man called
a foreigner
one hand on the nose of a horse
no taller than he was

and a cart behind them with wooden
wheels tight to the curb

by the streetcar tracks
were facing upstream waiting

on the cart a rocking
tower as big as a kitchen
with a round pointed roof
hung over the edges

yellow trellises all around
red painted chairs inside
one behind another
circling with music

the horse was small for the cart
the cart was small for the tower
the tower was small for the chairs
the chairs were small for us

the circle was large for the tower
the tower was large for the cart
the tower was large for the street
the street was large for us

but we sat in the music
and went round over nothing
as long as we could
and the streetcar came by

as we turned and it passed us
with faces at all the windows
looking out
knowing us

Photograph

After he died
they found the picture
that he had kept looking for
and had thought was lost
all those years

they did not know
how it had hung in the mind
of someone who could not find it
they did not even
know whose face
that was supposed to be

Unknown Forebear

Somebody who knew him
ninety years ago
called him by a name
he answered to
come out now they said to him
onto the porch and stand
right there

it was summer and the nine windows
that they could see
were open all the way
so was the front door
and the curtains faded as aprons hung
limp past the sills while he stood
there alone in his dark suit
and white beard in the sunshine

he appeared to know where he was
whose porch that was and whose
house behind him

younger than he was
and who had opened the windows

and who had left the ladder
propped in the branches up the lane
and the names of his children and their children
and the name of the place
with the pine tree out front
and the mullein a foot high growing
on the green bank
beyond the stones of the walk

as he stood still looking out
through the opening in the painted
picket fence
one tall picket one short picket
all the way along

and no gate in the opening

A Family

Would you believe me
if I told you the name of the farmers
at the end of the lake
where it grew shallow over the mossy rocks

and if you came in the morning the grass was blue
the fur of the rocks was wet the small frogs jumped
and the lake was silent behind you
except for echoes

you tied your boat carefully to a tree
before setting out across the cool pasture
watching for the bull
all the way to the barn

or if you came in the afternoon
the pasture glared and hummed the dark leaves smelled
from beside the water and the barn was drunk
by the time you got to it

to climb on the beams
to dive into the distant hay
will you believe
the names of the farmer's children

II

Shaving Without a Mirror

As though there could be more   than one center
many skies cleared in the night   and there it is
the mountain this face of it   still brindled with cloud shadows
if I raised my hand   I could touch it like air
high shallow valleys   cradling the clear wind
all like a thing remembered   where haystacks waited for winter

but now it is so blue   would there be eyes in it
looking out from dark nerves   as the morning passes in our time
while the sound of a plane rises   behind me beyond trees
so that I breathe and reach up to the air   and feel water
it is myself   the listener to the music
to the clouds in the gray passes   and the clear leaves

where are the forest voices   now that the forests have gone
and those from above the treeline   oh where that fed on fog
of a simpler compound   that satisfied them
when did I ever knowingly   set hands on a cloud
who have walked in one often   following the rim in anger
Brother the world is blind   and surely you come from it
where children grow steadily   without knowledge of creatures

other than domesticated   though rags of woods yet emerge
as the clouds part and sweep on   passing southward in spring
fingers crossing the slopes   shadows running leaping
all night that peak watched   the beacon over the sea
and answered nothing   now it turns to the morning
an expression of knowledge   above immigrant woods

nothing is native of fire   and everything is born of it
then I wash my face   as usual
trying to remember a date   before the war
coming to a green farm at sunrise   dew smell from pastures
after that there were various   graduations

this passion for counting   has no root of its own
I stand by a line of trees   staring at a bare summit
do I think I was born here   I was never born

Visitation

Two natives of the bare mountains   appear in the doorway
first I saw the dogs coming   far down the gold slope

the men shuffle and say hello   rimmed with sunlight
and ask if I've seen anything   up here all morning
winds of autumn are passing   over the uplands
migrations of shadows   crossing dry grass
clouds keep running the wall   of dark peaks to the south
ragged flocks trail   through the calling sky

but these had in mind   the animals
had I seen them at all   that made the hoofprints
or a sign of the hare   the quail or the partridge
no I tell them   and they nod and look away

how do I like it   up here they ask
but they won't come in   they were just passing
don't mind the dogs they say   and they tell me
the name of where they came from   and step from the doorway

every year they say   it's harder to find them
the animals   even up here
and I say is that true   and they laugh

The Red House

Room after room without a voice   no one to say
only another century   could afford so much space
spring sunlight through locked shutters   reveals the old
    patchworks
adrift on the old beds   in the dry air
and in the white fireplaces   already it is summer

but there is only one age   in all the rooms and mirrors
and it is beginning   it has come to begin
the sound of a bus arrives outside   and what looks like a closet
    door
in an upstairs bedroom opens   onto green woods
full of the thin leaves of May   and a shimmering meadow
and deep in grass   beyond a stream and a waterfall
the rusted windowless bus   to the amber fields

Tidal Lagoon

From the edge of the bare reef   in the afternoon
children who can't swim   fling themselves forward calling
and disappear for a moment   in the long mirror
that contains the reflections   of the mountains

Green Water Tower

A guest at Thanksgiving   said And you've got
a green water tower   with a blue two painted on it

it is there at the edge of the woods   on the hill to the east
at night it flattens   into the black profile of trees
clouds bloom from behind it   moonlight climbs through them
to the sound of pouring   far inside

in an east wind we wake hearing it   wondering where it is
above it the sky grows pale   white sun emerges
the green tower swells   in rings of shadow
day comes   we drink and stand listening

High Water

The river is rising   with the breathless sound of a fever
the wake along each shore   trembles and is torn away
a few steps up in the rain   rows of white faces
watch from the banks   backs to the cellar doors

behind the blue eyes   are the cellars' contents
silent in bottles   each with its date
on shelves waiting   under the dripping hats

when the faces draw closer   to each other in the rain
they talk like members   of one family
telling what could be moved   if they have to move it
saying where would be safe   talking of the gardens on the hills
the rains other years   what most needs repair
what the spring   means to the summer

even of the lake in the mountains   which they own together
and agree once again   never to sell

Line of Trees

Along the west of the woods   is a row of tall pines
the man who planted them   came from an island
thousands of miles to the south   and now with his wife
for a long time a nurse   but lately not right in the head
who came from an island   thousands of miles from his

he lives down the road   since their small house in the woods
burned beyond repair   but he still comes by
every so often   to ignore the mailbox
rusted sedan full of vines   brown fruit in the grassy ruts
and when he has gone a pheasant   barks from hiding
bird of a far continent   and whenever the boughs
part suddenly to reveal the yellow   house wall with its window
what they show is a mirror   full of western light

A House to the West

Day of harsh south wind built up the black clouds
but no rain fell and near sunset
the air turned still and full of afterlight

on the ridge to the west the tin barn in the trees
the well-digger's derrick
the plywood shack the color of clotted blood
settle onto the gray sky

the bony woman blond all her life
whose house that is
the woman named for a star
screams at her dog
calls baby talk to her goats
and far from the traffic where she was born
she turns into a shadow among fence posts

when the lovers and children had all got clear of her voice
she said of the red shack It is mine
and she got a driver to move it
one fine morning out onto the hill beyond everything
and then couldn't believe it
and never lights a lamp

The Cow

The two boys down the road   with a vegetable farm
they started from scratch   for their religion
say they didn't know anything   when they began
they had to pick it up   as they went along
all about growing things   and they made a lot of mistakes
said they never knew   much about animals
but their benefactor   bought these cows for the pasture
only the one is a bull   without any balls
and the one is a cow   but she's too young still
and the only one   that's been in milk
was Mama Cow   and they learned to milk her
and the whole three were got cheap   going to slaughter
and she wasn't considered   to be much of a milker
but they got most days   a gallon and a half
some days two   all through the summer
good milk too   better than what you buy
then the rains started   but it made no difference
there was a shed roof   all three could get under
but they all seemed to like   to hang out in the rain
just all the time   standing in the rain
then her milk all at once   began to go down
in a couple of days   it was right to nothing
then she got hold   of some dried apples they had
until she wouldn't   eat any more
and made it down   to the bottom of the pasture
to the mud hole   and lay down in the mud
and then couldn't get up   that's where they found her
she couldn't hardly   lift her head up
she was breathing heavy   they thought it was the apples
she looked so swollen   lying on her side
and she didn't get up   that whole day
so they sent for the vet   along late in the afternoon
he drove up   as the sun was going down
they opened the gate in the wires   at milking time
he brought the truck   into the pasture

he stepped down   at the edge of the mud
Picked a bad place to lie   lady he told her
listened to her all over   through a rubber tube
across the mud   and took her temperature
It wasn't the apples   he stood up and told them
she had pneumonia   weak with the fever
they'd have to move her   out of that mud there
they fastened to the horns first   and the truck tugged until a horn
    broke
he said he'd known a dragged horse   to leave all four hooves in
    the mud
they tried with the same rope   to the front legs and back legs
they dragged her along   to where it was anyways dry
he gave her some shots   showing them how
she tried to get up   but she fell right back
head down on the ground   on the broken horn
the moon at first quarter   gathering light
above the rain clouds   at the top of the hill
he said it was better   not to cover her
unless they were going   to sit up beside her
to keep the cover   from slipping off in the night
then he left   turning his lights on
in a few minutes   it started to rain
and they went out too   in a little while
to see a friend   and were not away long
but when they came back   she was gone lying there
she looked as though   she must be alive
with her eye open   in the moonlight
but when they touched her   it hit them for sure
Heavy they said   she was so big
they said they never   knew she was so big
and they saw dead things   every day
they couldn't believe it   at first they said
all the next morning   trying to burn her
with old tires   but they gave that up
and brought dirt   and piled it on her
That's what it's about   one of them said

Life and death isn't it   what it's about
and the other said   that after what they'd fed her
the blessings on the food   and the scriptures she'd heard
she was almost sure to be   reborn already
in human form   in a family of their faith

Questions to Tourists Stopped by a Pineapple Field

Did you like your piece of pineapple   would you like a napkin
who gave you the pineapple   what do you know about them
do you eat much pineapple   where you come from
how did this piece compare   with pineapple you have eaten
        before
what do you remember about the last time   you ate a piece of
        pineapple
did you know where it came from   how much did it cost
do you remember the first time   you tasted pineapple
do you like it better fresh   or from the can
what do you remember   of the picture on the can
what did you feel   as you looked at the picture
which do you like better   the picture or the pineapple field
did you ever imagine   pineapples growing somewhere

how do you like   these pineapple fields
have you ever seen   pineapple fields before
do you know whether pineapple   is native to the islands
do you know whether the natives   ate pineapple
do you know whether the natives   grew pineapple
do you know how the land was acquired   to be turned into
        pineapple fields
do you know what is done to the land   to turn it into pineapple fields
do you know how many months   and how deeply they plow it
do you know what those machines do   are you impressed
do you know what's in those containers   are you interested

what do you think was here   before the pineapple fields
would you suppose that the fields   represent an improvement
do you think they smell better   than they did before
what is your opinion   of those square miles of black plastic
where do you think the plastic   goes when the crop is over
what do you think becomes of the land   when the crop is over
do you think the growers know best   do you think this is for your
      own good

what and where was the last   bird you noticed
do you remember   what sort of bird it was
do you know whether   there were birds here before
are there any birds   where you come from
do you think it matters   what do you think matters more
have you seen any   natives since you arrived
what were they doing   what were they wearing
what language were they speaking   were they in nightclubs
are there any natives   where you come from

have you taken pictures   of the pineapple fields
would you like for me   to hold the camera
so that you can all   be in the picture
would you mind   if I took your picture
standing in front   of those pineapple fields
do you expect   to come back

what made you decide   to come here
was this what   you came for
when did you first   hear of the islands
where were you then   how old were you
did you first see the islands   in black and white
what words were used   to describe the islands
what do the words mean   now that you are here
what do you do   for a living
what would you say is   the color of pineapple leaves

when you look at things in rows   how do you feel
would you like to dream   of pineapple fields

is this your first visit   how do you like the islands
what would you say   in your own words
you like best   about the islands
what do you want   when you take a trip
when did you get here   how long will you be staying
did you buy any clothes   especially for the islands
how much did you spend on them   before you came
was it easy to find clothes   for the islands
how much have you spent on clothes   since you got here
did you make your own plans   or are you part of a group
would you rather be on your own   or with a group
how many are in your group   how much was your ticket
are the side-tours part of the ticket   or are they extra
are hotel and meals and car   part of the ticket or extra
have you already paid   or will you pay later
did you pay by check   or by credit card
is this car rented   by the day or week
how does it compare   with the one you drive at home
how many miles   does it do to a gallon
how far do you   want to go on this island

where have you been   in the last three hours
what have you seen   in the last three miles
do you feel hurried   on your vacation
are you getting   your money's worth
how old are you   are you homesick are you well
what do you eat here   is it what you want
what gifts are you planning   to take back
how much do you expect   to spend on them
what have you bought   to take home with you
have you decided   where to put each thing
what will you say   about where they came from
what will you say   about the pineapple fields

do you like dancing here   what do you do when it rains
was this trip   purely for pleasure
do you drink more   or less than at home
how do you like   the place where you live now
were you born there   how long have you lived there
what does the name mean   is it a growth community
why are you living there   how long do you expect to stay
how old is your house   would you like to sell it

in your opinion   coming from your background
what do the islands offer   someone of your age
are there any changes   you would like to promote
would you like to invest here   would you like to live here
if so would it be year round   or just for part of the year
do you think there is a future   in pineapple

The Briefcase

He came from the far north   I can name the country
gray hair cropped   to the shape of his skull
good gray suit   perfectly pressed
on his sharp shoulders   and from a long sleeve
thin hand in leather   hooked to a briefcase
and never looked at me   as he walked past
how then do I know   the voice and the accent
I've seen him before   from time to time
now I try to remember   what happened next each time
and I've heard what his work is   thinker and planner
administrator   of a model camp
what kind of camp   nobody could say
and he's on his way from there   right now as I watch him
disappear once more   behind a building
while leaves rustle   over my head
in the evening   and lights come on

Late Wonders

In Los Angeles the cars are flowing
through the white air
and the news of bombings

at Universal Studios
you can ride through an avalanche
if you have never
ridden through an avalanche

with your ticket
you can ride on a trolley
before which the Red
Sea parts
just the way it did
for Moses

you can see Los Angeles
destroyed hourly
you can watch the avenue named for somewhere else
the one on which you know you are
crumple and vanish incandescent
with a terrible cry
all around you
rising from the houses and families
of everyone you have seen all day
driving shopping talking eating

it's only a movie
it's only a beam of light

Going

Feet waiting in pairs   ways of sitting in subways
through all ages   ways of waiting
thinking of something else   that is elsewhere
iron carriages all day   flying through night
positions of daily papers   held up to be read
same papers flying in parks   rising above trees
are reflected once in glass   unknown glass
and in spilled water before   feet hurrying homeward

Standing Nowhere

When I come home in the city   and see the young roaches
running on the bare cliffs   they pause to see what I am
delaying their going   without company over unmapped spaces
feet finding their way   from black eggs small as dust
it is true that they do not know   anything about me
nor where we are from   we can have
little knowledge   we look at each other and wait
whatever we may do   afterward

Coming Back in the Spring

When I turn my head in the afternoon
there are the receding files
of tall buildings blue in the distance
with amber light along them ending
in amber light
and their sides shining above the river of cars
and I am home

here are the faces the faces
the cool leaves still lucent before summer

the voices
I am home before the lights come on
home when the thunder begins after dark
and the rain in the streets at night
while the iron train again
rumbles under the sidewalk
long cans full of light and
unseen faces disappearing
in my mind

many travelling behind the same headline
saying second
IRA hunger striker dies
in British hands in Ireland
and some ingesting the latest
smiling sentencing
from the face in the White House
whose syllables wither species and places
into deaths going on before us
as the print turns to the day's killings
around the planet

the words flowing under the place on the Avenue
where the truck ran over
two small boys at the intersection
Friday killing
both by the corner where the garden has been bulldozed
that flowered there for years
after the Loew's movie house was torn down
where the old pictures played

the trains rattle under the hooves
of the mounted police riding
down the Avenue at eleven in blue helmets
and past the iron skeleton
girders and stairs and sky

of the new tower risen
out of the gutted core
of St. Vincent's Hospital
most beautiful
of cities and most empty
pure Avenue behind the words of friends
and the known music

the stars are flaking in the apartment ceiling
and the lights of lives
are reflected crossing the floating night
the rain beats on the panes
above the Avenue
where I have watched it run
for twelve years in the spring
ambulances shriek among the trucks

this is an emergency the walkers
in the street in ones and twos
walk faster
those in groups walk more slowly
the white tower beyond Union Square
is lit up blue and white
during the first few
hours of darkness

we all sleep high off the ground

Happens Every Day

Right in midtown   walking in broad daylight
people around   and everything
all at once   this guy steps out
in front of him   and has a gun
grabs his briefcase   takes off with it

everybody around   is in a hurry
the first guy wakes up   to shout and the other one
starts running and the first guy   right after him
and the one with the briefcase   drops the gun
and the first guy   stops to pick it up
but people are passing   in between
he keeps on shouting   and barging through them
and the guy up ahead   drops the briefcase
so he starts after that   and sees somebody
gather up the gun   and get out of there
and when he stops where   he saw the briefcase
somebody else   has picked that up and gone
the other guy's vanished   and he stands looking
up and down the street   with the people
moving through him   from no beginning

Sheridan

The battle ended   the moment you got there

oh it was over it was over   in smoke
melted and the smoke still   washing the last away
of the shattered ends   the roaring fray
cannons gun carriages cavalry   fringes of infantry
seeping out of woods   blood bones breakage breaking
gone as though you   had just opened your eyes
and there was nobody   who saw what you had come to see
no face that realized   that you had arrived
no one in sight who knew   about you
how solid you were   General and how still
what were you doing   at last standing there
slightly smaller than life-size   in memory of yourself

this was certainly the place   there is no
place like this   this is the only place

it could have been   this unquestionably
is where the message came from   meant only for you
the touched intelligence rushing   to find you
tracing you gasping   drowning for lack of you
racing with shadows   of falling bodies
hunting you while the hours   ran and the first day
swung its long gates for cows   coming home to barnyards
fields were flooded with evening   seasons were resolved
forests came shouldering back   and the rounds
from the beginning   unrolled out of themselves
you were born and began to learn   what you learned
and it was going to find you   in your own time

with its torn phrases   to inform you
sir of your absence   to say it had happened
even then was happening   you were away
and they had broken upon   you they were long past
your picket lines they were at large   in your positions
outflanking outweighing   overrunning you
burning beyond your campfires   in your constellations
while the cows gave milk   and the country slept
and you continued there   in the crystal distance
you considered yours   until the moment
when the words turned it   to colored paper
then to painted glass   then to plain lantern glass
through which you could see   as you set your left
foot in the stirrup   the enemy
you had first imagined   flashing on the farmland

and what had become of   you all that while
who were you in the war   in the only night
then hands let go the black horse   the black road opened
all its miles   the stars on your coat went out
you were hurtling into the dark   and only the horse could see
I know because afterward   it was read to me
already in bed   my mother in the chair beside me

cellos in the avenue   of a lighted city
night after night again   I listened to your ride
as somebody never there   had celebrated it
and you did not see the road   on which you were going
growing out of itself   like a fingernail
you never saw the air   you were flying through
you never heard the hoofbeats   under you

all the way hearkening   to what was not there
one continuous mumbled   thunder collapsing
on endless stairs from   so far coming in the dark yet so
sure how could it have failed   to carry to you
calling finally by name   and how could you
in the meantime have heard nothing   but it was still not
that night's battle beyond its hills   that you were hearing
and attending to   bright before you
as a furnace mouth that kept falling   back forward away
filling with hands and known faces   that flared up and crumbled
in flowing coals   to rise then and form once more
and come on again living   so that you saw them
even when the crash of cannons   was close in the dawn
and day was breaking   all around you

a line of fence ran toward you   looking familiar
a shuttered house in the mist   you thought in passing
you remembered from some other time   so you seemed to know
where you were   my God the fighting
was almost to there already   you could hear
rifles echoing just down the road   and what sounded
like shouting and you could   smell it in the morning
where your own were watching for you   coming to meet you
horses neighing   and at once the night
had not happened behind you   the whole ride
was nothing out of which they   were hurrying you
on the white horse   telling you everything
that you had not seen could not see   never would see

taking you to the place   where you dismounted
and turned to look   at what you had come for

there was the smoke   and someone with your head
raised an arm toward it   someone with your mouth
gave an order   and stepped into the century
and is seen no more   but is said
to have won that battle   survived that war
died and been buried   and only you are there
still seeing it disappear   in front of you
everyone knows the place   by your name now
the iron fence   dry drinking fountain
old faces from brick buildings   out for some sun
sidewalk drunks   corner acquaintances
leaves luminous above you   in the city night
subway station   hands at green newsstand
traffic waiting   for the lights to change

The Fields

Saturday on Seventh Street
full-waisted gray-haired women in Sunday sweaters
moving through the tan shades of their booths
bend over cakes they baked at home
they gaze down onto the sleep of stuffed cabbages
they stir with huge spoons sauerkraut and potato dumplings
cooked as those dishes were cooked on deep
misty plains among the sounds of horses
beside fields of black earth on the other side of the globe
that only the oldest think they remember
looking down from their windows into the world
where everybody is now

none of the young has yet wept at the smell
of cabbages

those leaves all face
none of the young after long journeys
weeks in vessels
and staring at strange coasts through fog in first light
has been recognized by the steam of sauerkraut
that is older than anyone living
so on the street they play the music
of what they do not remember
they sing of places they have not known
they dance in new costumes under the windows
in the smell of cabbages from fields
nobody has seen

III

Palm

The palm is in no hurry
to be different
and it grows slowly
it knows how to be a palm
when it was a seed it knew
how to be a palm seed
when it was a flower
it knew how to be
the flower of a palm
when it was a palm it grew
slowly
and without eyes
in a salt wind

The Shore

How can anyone know that a whale
two hundred years ago could hear another
whale at the opposite end of the earth
or tell how long the eyes
of a whale have faced both halves of the world
and have found light far down in old company

with the sounds of hollow iron charging
clanging through the oceans and with the circuitries
and the harpoons of humans
and the poisoning of the seas
a whale can hear no farther through the present
than a jet can fly in a few minutes

in the days of their hearing the great Blues gathered like clouds
the sunlight under the sea's surfaces sank
into their backs as into the water around them

through which they flew invisible from above
except as flashes of movement
and they could hear each other's voices wherever they went

once it is on its own a Blue can wander
the whole world beholding both sides of the water
raising in each ocean the songs of the Blues
that it learned from distances it can no longer hear
it can fly all its life without ever meeting another Blue
this is what we are doing this is the way we sing oh Blue Blue

The Night Surf

Of tomorrow I have nothing to say
what I say is not tomorrow

tomorrow no animals
no trees growing at their will
no one in the White House
the words gone out

the end of our grasp and rage
and of our knowledge
what is between us and tomorrow

in the deep shade blue irises are open
we are barefoot in the airy house
after dark the surf roars on the cliffs

The Quoit

The iron ring
rose into the twilight
of late summer

the day still blue
no stars

it rose like a shadow
lit from underneath
the leaves were hanging motionless
on the big poplar
already full of night
and the voices had dropped at dusk

on a table by a new window
in an old house with no lights on
a black metal panther
glared through the black hollyhocks
toward the group of men standing under floodlamps
beside four boxes of wet clay

they had a right to their game
on coal company property
that could not be built on
in case the company
needed to sink a shaft to the mine
in a hurry

those years often the nights smelled of autumn
and people said to each other in the mornings
did you hear it last night
late
was it blasting again someone would ask
no someone else would answer
it was pickaxes

The Middle of Summer

By now you have envisaged
in lives as many as those
of a tree in spring
the summer nights
in the cabin by the lake
with the sun never setting

the fire on the beach
through the endless hours of sunset
and have held the sound of the north dome
of the planet turning
gazing constantly at the sun

the lull of the lakes at that
time the hum of the surfaces
the breath of woods
bird voices clattering
through the sleepless light
of the sun at midnight
and your long shadow walking
on the still water

that is what you go on seeing
at that latitude
as the water turns silent and then
begins to tremble

James

News comes that a friend far away
is dying now

I look up and see small flowers appearing
in spring grass outside the window
and can't remember their name

Berryman

I will tell you what he told me
in the years just after the war
as we then called
the second world war

don't lose your arrogance yet he said
you can do that when you're older
lose it too soon and you may
merely replace it with vanity

just one time he suggested
changing the usual order
of the same words in a line of verse
why point out a thing twice

he suggested I pray to the Muse
get down on my knees and pray
right there in the corner and he
said he meant it literally

it was in the days before the beard
and the drink but he was deep
in tides of his own through which he sailed
chin sideways and head tilted like a tacking sloop

he was far older than the dates allowed for
much older than I was he was in his thirties
he snapped down his nose with an accent
I think he had affected in England

as for publishing he advised me
to paper my wall with rejection slips
his lips and the bones of his long fingers trembled
with the vehemence of his views about poetry

he said the great presence
that permitted everything and transmuted it
in poetry was passion
passion was genius and he praised movement and invention

I had hardly begun to read
I asked how can you ever be sure
that what you write is really
any good at all and he said you can't

you can't you can never be sure
you die without knowing
whether anything you wrote was any good
if you have to be sure don't write

A Birthday

Something continues and   I don't know what to call it
though the language is full of suggestions
in the way of language
                              but they are all anonymous
and it's almost your birthday   music next to my bones

these nights we hear the horses   running in the rain
it stops and the moon comes out   and we are still here

the leaks in the roof go on dripping   after the rain has passed
smell of ginger flowers   slips through the dark house
down near the sea   the slow heart of the beacon flashes

the long way to you is still tied to me   but it brought me to you
I keep wanting to give you   what is already yours
it is the morning   of the mornings together
breath of summer   oh my found one
the sleep in the same current   and each waking to you

when I open my eyes   you are what I wanted to see

The Sea Cliffs at Kailua in December

Down on the tongue of black rock
where the long waves break
a young woman stands with a baby named Mist
we sit in the sun by the crag
spray blowing high into the fans of the hala trees
friends talk of how the age that is ours
came to the islands
where there were kings
in a few hours none of us will be here
the voices of the children fly up from rock pools
clouds move in from the sea
voices grow distant
a bright fish gasps on a stone near the fire
there are ghosts in the steep valley
through the years we have been along the wild coast
headland by headland
but never here

Ali

Small dog named for a wing
never old and never young

abandoned with your brothers on a beach
when you were scarcely weaned

taken home starving
by one woman with
too many to feed as it was

handed over to another
who tied you out back in the weeds
with a clothesline and fed you if she remembered

on the morning before the eclipse of the moon
I first heard about you over the telephone

only the swellings of insect bites
by then held the skin away from your bones

thin hair matted filthy the color of mud
naked belly crusted with sores
head low frightened silent watching

I carried you home and gave you milk and food
bathed you and dried you

dressed your sores and sat with you
in the sun with your wet head on my leg

we had one brother of yours already
and had named him for the great tree of the islands
we named you for the white shadows
behind your thin shoulders

and for the reminder of the desert
in your black muzzle lean as an Afghan's

and for the lightness of your ways
not the famished insubstance of your limbs

but even in your sickness and weakness
when you were hobbled with pain and exhaustion

an aerial grace a fine buoyancy
a lifting as in the moment before flight

I keep finding why that is your name

the plump vet was not impressed with you
and guessed wrong for a long time
about what was the matter

so that you could hardly eat
and never grew like your brother

small dog wise in your days

never servile never disobedient
and never far

standing with one foot on the bottom stair
hoping it was bedtime

standing in the doorway looking up
tail swinging slowly below sharp hip bones

toward the end you were with us whatever we did

the gasping breath through the night
ended an hour and a half before daylight

the gray tongue hung from your mouth
we went on calling you holding you

feeling the sudden height

The School on the Roof

Up there day and night for weeks   they turn to water
turn themselves into water   of day water of night
clouds travel across them   rain vanishes into them
when wind stops they grow clear   birds come and are gone in
        them
sun rises and sets in them   their stars come out
until they come down   come down
some all the colors   of lakes and rivers
some so you can't   see them at all

Going from the Green Window

Saying to the square that is always open good-bye
is uprooting my own foot
I never remembered the root starting
there is nothing to say good-bye to

In a room of wind and unabiding
in midair like a leg walking
in a turning place where boxes have stayed packed for years
where in storms the walls bleed
over the flooded floors
where at all hours constellations
of black cows wait round about
growing on the hill of grass

I watch through dark leaves once
those shadows in the day pasture
moving slowly to drink on the way to the big tree
this morning

The Truth of Departure

With each journey it gets
worse
what kind of learning is that
when that is what we are born for

and harder and harder to find
what is hanging on
to what
all day it has been raining
and I have been writing letters
the pearl curtains
stroking the headlands
under immense dark clouds
the valley sighing with rain
everyone home and quiet

what will become of all these
things that I see
that are here and are me
and I am none of them
what will become
of the bench and the teapot
the pencils and the kerosene lamps
all the books all the writing
the green of the leaves
what becomes of the house

and the island
and the sound of your footstep

who knows it is here
who says it will stay
who says I will know it
who said it would be all right

One Night

I ride a great horse climbing
    out of a rose cloud
        onto a black cinder mountain

long ago and a horn is blowing
    and far ahead the light
        answers

Émigré

You will find it is
much as you imagined
in some respects
which no one can predict
you will be homesick
at times for something you can describe
and at times without being able to say
what you miss
just as you used to feel when you were at home

some will complain from the start
that you club together
with your own kind
but only those who have

done what you have done
conceived of it longed for it
lain awake waiting for it
and have come out with
no money no papers nothing
at your age
know what you have done
what you are talking about
and will find you a roof and employers

others will say from the start
that you avoid
those of your country
for a while
as your country becomes
a category in the new place
and nobody remembers the same things
in the same way
and you come to the problem
of what to remember after all
and of what is your real
language
where does it come from what does it
sound like
who speaks it

if you cling to the old usage
do you not cut yourself off
from the new speech
but if you rush to the new lips
do you not fade like a sound cut off
do you not dry up like a puddle
is the new tongue to be trusted

what of the relics of your childhood
should you bear in mind pieces

of dyed cotton and gnawed wood
lint of voices untranslatable stories
summer sunlight on dried paint
whose color continues to fade in the
growing brightness of the white afternoon
ferns on the shore of the transparent lake
or should you forget them
as you float between ageless languages
and call from one to the other who you are

What is Modern

Are you modern

is the first
tree that comes
to mind modern
does it have modern leaves

who is modern after hours
at the glass door
of the drugstore
or
within sound of the airport

or passing the
animal pound
where once a week I
gas the animals
who is modern in bed

when
was modern born
who first was pleased
to feel modern

who first claimed the word
as a possession
saying I'm
modern

as someone might say
I'm a champion
or I'm
famous or even
as some would say I'm
rich

or I love the sound
of the clarinet
yes so do I
do you like classical
or modern

did modern
begin to be modern
was there a morning
when it was there for the first time
completely modern

is today modern
the modern sun rising
over the modern roof
of the modern hospital
revealing the modern water tanks and aerials
of the modern horizon

and modern humans
one after the other
solitary and without speaking
buying the morning paper
on the way to work

Direction

All I remember of the long lecture
which is all I remember of one summer
are the veins on the old   old bald head
and the loose white sleeve   and bony finger pointing
beyond the listeners
over their heads

there was the dazzling   wall and the empty sunlight
and reaching out of his age he told them
for the last time
what to do when they got to the world
giving them his every breath   to take with them like water
as they vanished

nobody was coming back that way

The New Season

On the third night of autumn
hearing rats in the dry
brush and leaves under the big trees
below the house
I go down with one of the dogs
to frighten them away

where the end of the house
looms high off the ground
we look down the dark slope
with a flashlight
listening
what was it
old dog old good heart
old Roland not too bright
only one eye

in the black
blossoms go on falling
from the Christmasberry trees
like the dripping after rain
small unseen colorless
blossoms ticking
but the bees are not there

worms are awake under the leaves
beetles are awake eating
upside down in the dark
leaves are awake hearing
in the complete night

I stand with a flashlight
in a smell of fruit
and we wait

Hearing

Back when it took all day to come up
from the curving broad ponds on the plains
where the green-winged jaçanas ran on the lily pads

easing past tracks at the mouths of gorges
crossing villages silted in hollows
in the foothills
each with its lime-washed church by the baked square
of red earth and its
talkers eating fruit under trees

turning a corner and catching
sight at last of inky forests far above
steep as faces
with the clouds stroking them and the glimmering
airy valleys opening out of them

waterfalls still roared from the folds
of the mountain
white and thundering and spray drifted
around us swirling into the broad leaves
and the waiting boughs

once I took a tin cup and climbed
the sluiced rocks and mossy branches beside
one of the high falls
looking up step by step into
the green sky from which rain was falling
when I looked back from a ledge there were only
dripping leaves below me
and flowers

beside me the hissing
cataract plunged into the trees
holding on I moved closer
left foot on a rock in the water
right foot on a rock in deeper water
at the edge of the fall
then from under the weight of my right foot
came a voice like a small bell ringing
over and over one clear treble
syllable

I could feel it move
I could feel it ring in my foot in my skin
everywhere
in my ears in my hair
I could feel it in my tongue and in the hand
holding the cup
as long as I stood there it went on
without changing

when I moved the cup
still it went on

when I filled the cup
in the falling column
still it went on
when I drank it rang in my eyes
through the thunder curtain

when I filled the cup again
when I raised my foot
still it went on
and all the way down
from wet rock to wet rock
green branch to green branch
it came with me

until I stood
looking up and we drank
the light water
and when we went on we could
still hear the sound
as far as the next turn on the way over

The Black Jewel

In the dark
there is only the sound of the cricket

south wind in the leaves
is the cricket
so is the surf on the shore
and the barking across the valley

the cricket never sleeps
the whole cricket is the pupil of one eye
it can run it can leap it can fly
in its back the moon
crosses the night

there is only one cricket
when I listen

the cricket lives in the unlit ground
in the roots
out of the wind
it has only the one sound

before I could talk
I heard the cricket
under the house
then I remembered summer

mice too and the blind lightning
are born hearing the cricket
dying they hear it
bodies of light turn listening to the cricket
the cricket is neither alive nor dead
the death of the cricket
is still the cricket
in the bare room the luck of the cricket
echoes

INDEX

Book design by John D. Berry Design. Composition by Typeworks. The text type is Monotype Bembo, a digitized version of the modern revival of a typeface originally cut by Francesco Griffo for the Venetian publisher Aldus Manutius, and used to print Cardinal Bembo's *De Ætna* in 1495. The display type is Poetica, an Adobe Originals typeface designed by Robert Slimbach in 1992 and modeled on formal chancery handwriting scripts of the Italian Renaissance. *Printed by McNaughton & Gunn.*